My Journey to the Light through Divine Encounters

My Journey to the Light through Divine Encounters

JONATHAN EMMANUEL DAVIS

Softcover ISBN: 979-8-9895655-3-5

Library of Congress Cataloging-in-Publication Data

Names: Davis, Jonathan Emmanuel
Title: Road To Damascus/Jonathan Emmanuel Davis
Library of Congress Control Number: 2024900166

Jonathan Emmanuel Davis
Grand Prairie, TX 75052

Cover Design by Abiodun T.
Editing by 302 Designs Co.

THRIVE Revolution Publishing
Daytona Beach, FL

DEDICATION

To Jesus, my Lord and Savior, the inspiration behind the book. He has been with me through the darkest of times of my life.

To the person of the Holy Spirit who is my best friend and constant companion.

ACKNOWLEDGEMENT

I would like to acknowledge my wonderful wife Mojana Davis, who helped me write this book. Without her, this book would not have been written. I would also like to acknowledge everyone that has made it to the book and has been a part of my journey.

Contents

INTRODUCTION

Greetings

For sometime now God has pressed upon my heart to share my life's testimony. After many months of wrestling with God about it I finally submitted. I have traveled a long and windy dark road to get to the light. I want to take you along my life's journey. Over the course of my Journey, I have experienced many roadblocks from the age of 4 through the age of 26. I have also had many victories. There's certain roadblocks and checkpoints that we all must go through in life. Every butterfly starts out as a caterpillar, and every caterpillar becomes a butterfly. It doesn't matter how messy your story seems, eventually we metamorph into who God wants us to be. The stages of life can sometimes be overbearing and seem as if there's no end in sight. I am here to tell you there's light at the end of the tunnel.

PHASE 1

1997

When I was five, my mother left me. I still remember that hot summer day when my brother and I were outside playing basketball with no shoes on and the next thing you know there was a white thunderbird pulling up to my grandmother's house. To my surprise, it was my dad.

"Go, go, go pack your clothes," I remember him telling me. I dreaded every minute of packing. I didn't want to leave my brother and grandmother, afterall she was my favorite person in the world. By the look on my father's face, I could tell he meant business.

"You done yet?" he yelled from the living room.

"Yes sir, I'm almost done", I replied.

After packing my bags, I slowly made my way to the living room. My father then reached his hand into his pocket, opened his wallet and proceeded to hand my brother $100. I was always jealous because my dad always gave my brother money and not me and I never understood why.

I waved goodbye to my grandmother and my brother; and my father and I drove off. While driving in the car, I didn't say much. I stared out the window thinking when would I see my grandmother and brother again.

"What's on your mind?", my dad asked.

"Oh nothing" I replied.

I could tell he knew something was wrong and besides I didn't have the courage to tell him that I didn't want to leave. After about maybe 20 minutes of driving, we finally made it to Marrero and I brought my bags inside. All my step brothers and sisters were outside waiting for me. I hated being at that place. Being the youngest, I was always getting picked on and getting made fun of for the way I looked and for my mother not being present. I tried not to let things they said get the best of me, so I played it off, but deep down inside, I felt every bit of it. I mean after all, this was my reality, my mother was nowhere in sight and quite frankly, I was tired of defending her.

As a child, I always wondered where she was, why she left, and if she loved me. Being an introverted child, I never talked much so I didn't feel the need or feel comfortable talking to someone about the situation I was in, so I talked to God instead. I felt he always listened to me and for some odd reason, I always felt Him next to me. He would always comfort me and I felt He understood me when no one else did.

THAT ONE TIME

After transitioning to my dad's house, I only spent summers with my brother and grandmother while spending the remainder of the year with my father. I begged my father to let me move with my grandmother, but he repeatedly said no; I was his responsibility. With my mother leaving, my dad wanted to make sure I was always protected. He tried to protect me from any more hurt. I didn't have the courage to ask him why my mother left so I didn't bother asking.

I remember two days before Christmas when I was 10 years old and my dad told me my mother was coming to town. I was leaping for joy inside, I could not believe it. I was smiling ear to ear and I felt like I was on top of the world. Although I was really excited about it, I could tell my dad wasn't too fond about it and I didn't understand why. I'm sure it was his way of protecting me. My dad wasn't a man that wore his emotions on his sleeve, but when he felt strongly about something, he made sure you knew of it.

"You got all your stuff?"

"Yes sir, I got it all," I replied.

"You know you always forget stuff, I don't want to have to turn the car around," said Dad.

"Hey grandma!"

"Hey baby," she replied with her cajun accent.

"Where is Tyrone?" I asked.

"Oh he's in the back playing the game."

"Okay!" I responded.

So I walked to the backroom to join in.

"What's up bro?"

He nodded his head, "what's up?"

My brother always had a funny way of showing that he was happy to see me. Deep down I knew he was just as happy as I was to see him.

"You talked to mom?" I asked.

"No, I haven't, but she's on her way," he responded.

That put a big smile on my face.

"Whatchu smiling' about?" he asked.

"Oh, I'm just happy to see her, aren't you?"

"I mean not really, it is what it is," he responded.

He said it so harshly, and I could tell he meant it. With both parents missing, I could tell my brother grew numb to being separated from his parents. My mom was nowhere to be found, and his dad had been in jail his entire life.

Growing up I was always envious of my brother. At the time I didn't know my brother was envious of me … and everything that I had.

It never dawned on me that he was living in a single parent home with his grandmother as the parent. By the look of things, it seemed like he had it made. He always had the latest shoes, clothes, and games. You name it, he had it. Not to mention, he was able to stay out as late as he wanted to.

What I didn't know was that my grandmother was overcompensating by buying him gifts for the trauma my brother was experiencing to make him happy, but in reality it was like putting a bandage on an open womb and it only made it worse.

While I was complaining that my brother had more than me, in his mind I had it made.

* * *

Boom boom boom! I heard a knock on the door! My heart started beating out of my chest, is it really her?! I rushed towards the door to open it.

"Who is it," I yelled.

"It's your cousin Brandon."

"Ughhh!" I sighed. "Really?", I thought.

"Come on in.", I said as I wave my hand toward the inside of the house.

"Did Tyra Make it in yet," Brandon asked.

"No she hasn't, we're still waiting."

"Okay," he replied, "I'll just wait until she gets here."

About two hours passed and I waited by the front door. I thought of all the things I would ask and say to her.

Knock, Knock!

"Who is it?" I yelled.

"Tyra!" I proceeded to open the door. "Hey my baby, how are you?"

"I'm good. I was just up waiting on you," I replied.

"Come help me get these bags out of the car," she responded.

"Okay."

"Where's your brother?"

"He's inside with Brandon playing the game," I replied.

I can't lie, it was really awkward for me. As strange as it may sound I didn't know how to act around my own mother. I was so nervous to even say anything to her, but there's something about her that made me feel so connected to her. After grabbing the rest of the bags, we headed inside to eat dinner and watch a movie. I suggested the *Five Heartbeats;* it was my favorite movie . After about 20 minutes into the movie I could feel myself nodding off. Next thing you know I was out cold snoring like a baby.

In the middle of the night I felt someone cuddle up next to me. It was my mother. I felt her right next to me. It was the closest we've ever been. I can still remember that moment. It was one of the best nights of my life.

* * *

Before you know it, it was Christmas day and we were all gathered in the living room opening gifts. This was my brother and my first time having Christmas with my mother. We opened one gift after another, and I got everything I had asked for. I was all smiles, but my brother didn't look so happy. He opened the gifts that my mother got him and he also had gifts his father sent him from prison. He opened up the box with his name written on it and pulled out a handmade leather belt with his name on it. As he pulled the belt out, I noticed he showed no emotions. I was more happy for him than he was.

"Do y'all like your gifts?" my mom asked.

"Yes! I loved it," I said.

After spending hours opening gifts, eating, playing games and enjoying family, my mother left the next day.

"Beep, beep!" My dad was honking his horn waiting for me. I felt a wave of emotions and I didn't know whether to cry, or run away. On one hand I had my mother leaving me again and on the other hand I was leaving my brother and grandmother again. I felt my Christmas was ruined. I remember that long ride home praying to God, asking Him to give me comfort, confidence and begging him to stay with me to fill the void of my mother not being there.

GONE WITH THE WIND

I was going into my sixth grade year when Hurricane Katrina hit my city of New Orleans. In the past, during hurricane season, we never evacuated because more often than not, hurricanes got diverted in a different direction. For some strange reason, my stepmother felt the need to evacuate this time around.

After my first day of school ended, we packed our bags and headed for Ft. Worth, Texas. By the time we arrived in Houston, Hurricane Katrina had already taken a toll on the city of New Orleans.

While dining in Waffle House, you could literally feel the rain and winds of the storm. After about an hour had passed, we got back in the car and headed to Ft. Worth. After waking up from a short night's rest, I woke up to screaming, yelling, and crying from my relatives. I got out of bed to see what all the commotion was about and when I walked in the living room, my family was gathered around the TV and for the first time in my life, my city of New Orleans was destroyed. It looked like something off a horror movie. The only thing that I could think of was, "is my family okay?"

My older sister decided she wanted to stay behind even though my father begged her to come. I can still feel the emotions of that catastrophic moment. After about two weeks, my family and I decided to go back home to get the rest of our belongings. At this time, there was a curfew issued in the state of Louisiana, so we decided to get on the road early so we could make it in time before curfew. Unfortunately, due to traffic, we were running behind schedule. We got to New Orleans at about 8 o'clock at night and as we drove into the city it was pitch black. You couldn't see anything. The storm had completely wiped out all electricity. As we drove about 20 mph due to debris in the middle of the road, when I looked out of the car window, there were buildings tumbled over, billboard signs in the middle of streets, gas stations ruined, shattered glass from corporate buildings, and power lines hanging from the rooftops. We were about a mile away from our home and we saw the first headlights from another car.

Immediately, we cut off the car lights and parked the car because we weren't supposed to be out after curfew. As the headlights approached us, I noticed that it was a tank, and it was the national guard. We waited for about 10 minutes after the car passed and drove up to our house. The first thing we noticed was that our front door was kicked in and as we walked into the house, our furniture was missing along with other belongings. We packed up what little we could and headed across the street to my grandparents.

I still remember having trouble falling asleep because of how hot it was in the house due to no electricity. I had to open the front door to get whatever air I could. Later the next morning, we headed back to Ft. Worth Texas. I was sad because I didn't get a chance to see my brother or my grandmother. For some strange reason, I felt like it was going to be awhile before I would see them again. Before Katrina devastated the city of New Orleans, I made a lot of new friendships at school that I was excited about. Not to mention, my best friend, Ashton, was still in New Orleans and I wondered if I would ever see him again. Riding in the car, I was filled with so many emotions and I felt like it was deja vu. Either someone or something was given to me, and after a short while it was taken away repeatedly. I often wondered, if I'd ever go back to New Orleans.

After we arrived back to Ft. Worth, a couple weeks passed, and we were getting ready to enroll in school. I remember walking into Creekview Middle school and for the first time, I was the only black person in the room. I never felt so out of place in my life. I mean just being in Texas was all very new to me.

Growing up, I loved watching western movies and that shaped my idea of Texas, people living in the country, raising cattle, and thriving in agriculture. Besides, the last movie I saw in the theatre was *Texas Chainsaw Massacre* and it was based on a true story, so Texas was not the place I wanted to be.

On my first day of school, before my first period class, I was called into the principal's office. When I got there she told me to write down everything I wanted, so I wrote down just about everything. The list included video games, clothes, shoes, and a bike. Finally, I felt like God was answering my prayers.

After about a week , I was called back to the principal's office to collect my gifts. I was all smiles walking to the office. Mr. Thurman handed me a big bag and told me to open it. When I looked inside the bag, it was socks, boxers, Haines t-shirts, and some goodies. I tried not to be ungrateful, but they didn't give me anything I asked for. I guess God didn't answer my prayers after all.

Later that day, throughout my third period PE course, it was time for me to sign up for football. This was the highlight of my day. God knows I love me some football! After a month had passed by, it was almost football season and I was issued my first football equipment. This was the happiest I had ever been since Hurricane Katrina. Before you know it, we made it to our first practice and let's just say by the end of the day, after running circles around my teammates, I felt like Boobie Miles in Friday *Night Lights.*

SILENT CRIES

One day after leaving school, I got a phone call from my older sister Joh'eisha.

"Hey did you hear the news?"

"No, I haven't," I replied.

"Your brother just went to jail and he's gonna be in there for a while."

I felt my heart sink to the bottom of my chest. Here we go again, feeling like I can never escape disappointment. When I got home, I went into my room and cried for hours. I had so many questions for God. "Why is this happening to me? Why do I always have to go through this? When am I going to catch a break?"

After hours of crying, I felt the peace of God come over me and I looked to the corner of my bed, picked up my football, and started tossing it in the air. I slowly felt the pain going away. I couldn't think about anything but going to practice the next day. At the time, I didn't know how therapeutic football was to me. Growing up in an African-American household, mental health was not discussed and , I didn't know what depression was. All I knew was playing football made me feel better about any and every situation. There were times where I wanted to express to my parents how I felt, but I couldn't muster up the courage to do so. I went to God instead.

About a month and a half had gone by since my brother went to jail and I got some more bad news. I got home from school and my dad called me into the living room and told me that my grandmother had passed away.

I was devastated. My grandmother and I had such a tight relationship. I can't describe in words how close we were. This was the worst pain of my life. I remember sitting on the stairs of my apartment asking God to take me with her. Yet again, I found myself asking God "why me? Why do I always have to go through this? When are the tables going to turn?"

One week had gone by, and after talking to close relatives, my family were preparing for the funeral. I asked myself, "why hasn't my daddy said anything about taking me to the funeral?" I didn't have the courage to ask my dad why he wasn't taking me to my grandmother's funeral, but unfortunately, he didn't take me.

I found myself backed up against the wall with no one to run to, no one to talk to but God. It felt like deja vu all over again, sitting in my bed, tossing a football up in the air. Weeks had gone by since my grandmother's passing and I was still hurting but no one knew it. I had a way of covering things up, smiling on the outside but crying on the inside. Only God truly knew the pain I felt. For some strange reason, I felt no pain while on the football field. (It was as if God was healing me through football.)

THE INTRODUCTION

In 2008, I started the next phase of my life. I entered into my first year of high school. I was excited for what was up ahead. Besides, I was tired of middle school and after going to countless high school football games, I was ready to play with the big boys. At this stage in my life, I was going through puberty and girls became more and more attractive to me. I got into my first real relationship in high school. If you asked me, I just knew I was in love, but my parents - they would've said, "boy you don't even know what love is."

"Make sure you're not getting distracted from homework and football," my dad would tell me.

"Ahh dad c'mon you know I got this," I would often tell him.

"Alright, alright. As soon as your grades start slippin' I'ma pull you off of that football team," my dad responded.

A few weeks into high school, I felt like I was on top of the world. Even though I was a freshman, I was the star athlete of my high school and there was nothing you could tell me about it. Every now and then, I would think about how much I missed my brother and how I would never see my grandmother again, well not until I get to heaven at least.

I remember walking over to my girlfriend's house from school and we were rushing to get there before her parents got home. I mean, I was a virgin , but where I come from, being a virgin wasn't something to brag about. After about 20 minutes of walking, we finally made it to her house. We opened the backdoor and headed upstairs to her room. When I entered her room, I felt really uneasy. I felt like God was literally pulling on me not to go in there, but on the other hand, I felt such an urge to have sex.

Before you know it, I was laying on the bed and she was on top of me kissing me. I didn't have the courage to go all the way, so we dry humped instead. How pointless was that?! Fifteen minutes had gone by and we heard her parents pull up in the driveway. We immediately rushed downstairs to cut on the TV and act like nothing was happening.

"Hey Jonathan!" her dad yelled, "how are you?"

"I'm doing good, I thought I would stop by the house since I was in the neighborhood."

"You're welcomed to come by anytime," he replied.

I was surprised he didn't ask me about sports since that's what most of our conversations were about. At times it seemed as if he felt his daughter was privileged to date me. I didn't understand why. I felt like I was just a regular Joe. A few hours had gone by and we were all downstairs laughing and playing games around the kitchen table. I leaned over to my girlfriend and told her it was time for me to leave. I could just feel my dad calling me at any moment telling me to come home. I didn't have a car so my girlfriend volunteered to take me home.

When I got to my house I remembered a conversation some of my teammates were having about pornography in the locker room. At the time, I had no idea what it was, so I decided that I would do some research. I waited until about 12 a.m., when everybody fell asleep, logged onto my parents' computer. Let's just say about 30 min later my eyes were glued to the computer screen. I went from one video to the next, before you know it my hands were in my pants and the rest was history.

"Beeep! Beeep! Beeep!" my alarm was going off the next morning. I struggled to get out of bed. I was never a morning person. I rolled over and thought to myself, "did that really just happen?". It was a pretty bold move watching pornography in my parents' living room. I knew if my dad ever caught me, he would kill me. While I was at school, I couldn't stop thinking about it. I was at lunch with my girlfriend and couldn't stop imagining what she looked like with her clothes off. At the time I couldn't wait to get home to watch it again.

One night turned into a week, and before you knew it weeks turned into months. It seemed like I couldn't go a day without watching it. I noticed when I opened the door to pornography that everything about me had changed. It affected every area of my life. I noticed the way I saw my girlfriend and women changed. I also saw a major decline in my academic life, and I slept a whole lot more. Even my relationship with God took a major turn. Whenever I had a problem at home with my parents, or if I was grieving the loss of my grandmother I would watch pornography. In my mind it was a quick fix and gave me an excuse to not have to talk to anyone, but I would just express myself and get the release I needed while watching it. Even though my porn addiction was at an all-time high, I always felt God telling me to stop doing it. I ignored that until the 'voice' went away, and over time my heart grew numb to it. When I look back at it, pornography took the place of God in my life.

MANIFESTATION

In 2012, I finally entered into my senior year of high school. Things were great for me. I was thriving in every area of my life, and most importantly I had football offers coming in left and right. It seemed like every day I was getting pulled out of class to speak with college coaches. It felt like all the hard work I put in both on and off the field was finally paying off. Even better, with only four classes, I had early dismissal.

One day after talking to Texas Christian University, I went out to the football field and I sat and prayed. I asked God not to take football away from me. I didn't want to get too excited because it felt like every time I got ready to walk through a door, it was closed in my face. I felt like football was all I had and I wanted to make my dream of going to the NFL come through for my brother and me. Since we were kids, we aspired of playing professionally, but with my brother in jail, I felt the burden to carry the torch alone.

Six years had passed since I talked to my brother. I felt so bad, at times I blamed myself for him being in jail. Also at times, I blamed my mother because she wasn't there for him. During that long heartfelt prayer, I felt God tugging on my heart to forgive my mother for abandoning me. I was perplexed because I never got answers as to why she left. I was even more upset that she never came to one of my football games. There were moments when I would grieve because I saw my teammates' parents at their games and my mother was never in attendance. My dad, however, was always at my games, but for some reason I always wished my mother was there with him.

After I finished praying, I left the field and headed to meet my friends at my house. We all had plans to go out that night and hang with some girls from a nearby school. By this time, my girlfriend and I had broken up. I wasn't much of a partier, so I didn't go out much in high school. Besides, I was into older women. I was infatuated with mature women that were older than me. At the time I didn't know that this was a coping mechanism for my mother not being in my life. I thought I was just naturally attracted to them, but that wasn't the case.

Later that night, while at the party, I felt uneasy and out of place. I decided to leave the party early and go home. When I got home, I sat up and played video games before I went to bed. I had a big playoff game the next day and I had 15 schools confirmed to be at my playoff game.

Before you know it, it was 6 a.m. and my alarm clock was going off. I jumped up out of bed, headed to the kitchen to make some breakfast. I wanted to make sure I was fueled for the big day.

"You ready?" my dad asked.

"I was born ready," I replied.

"Alright let's go," he responded.

Thank God I had early dismissal because the last thing I wanted to do was sit in class all day when I had a big playoff game. Three o'clock came quickly and we all loaded onto the bus headed to Brewer Stadium for the game. I was so hype when I walked in the locker room. We all had new helmets and uniforms. If it's one thing you know about me, I always like to be the flyest person on the field. My favorite player was Dieon Sanders and Dieon always said "look good, feel good, and when you feel good, you play good."

Midway through the second quarter, I was running down the sideline and felt a sharp pain in my hamstring. Immediately, I fell to the ground and began to gasp for air. The entire stadium was completely silent and by the looks on my teammates face, they all looked defeated seeing that I was hurt. I felt this pain before and I knew I pulled my hamstring. I headed toward the sideline with the help of my teammates. My athletic trainer gave me a bag of ice and some ibuprofen to stop the swelling. I was full of emotions, I reached over by the bench, grabbed the towel and through it over my face. I didn't want anyone to see me cry and I didn't want my teammates to be discouraged. Immediately, I started praying and I started asking God, "why? Why is this happening to me?"

I felt like I was going backwards again. I took a moment and looked into the crowd and I saw all the college coaches that came to see me. At that moment, I felt like my career was taking a turn for the worse. Half-time came and we were still up by 10 points. When I got in the locker room, I started moving my hamstring around again. I was determined to get back in the game. While my coach was giving a halftime speech, I was praying under my breath, "God please, heal me." I tore my hamstring before and it took about 4 months for me to recover. I sat out all of spring ball going into my senior year because of it. A few moments later, we headed back down to the field to start the second half. While sitting on the table, I felt heat on my lower hamstring while I was praying. A few moments later, I got up and started jogging.

I leaned over and told my trainer, "I think my hamstring is fine. I think I'm ready to go back into the game."

He looked at me like I was crazy. He said, "are you sure?"

"Yes sir, I am," I responded.

Then he looked at me and said, "let me re-examine your hamstring, go and sprint down the sideline."

I did exactly what he asked and I took off sprinting. I looked into the crowd and I could see my dad praying. I couldn't believe it. My hamstring felt good as new. We were two minutes into the 4th quarter when I got back into the game. We called a timeout and the coach called my number. I was gasping for air, "well here goes nothing," I told myself. After we broke the huddle, I got back in the game and my quarterback threw me the ball. I ran in it for a touchdown. I ran over to the crowd and started pumping them up. We were down 10 points, but I just knew that we were getting ready to make a comeback. At this point, we had the momentum on our side and we started making plays one after another. My coach called my number two more times, and I scored two more touchdowns to steal the victory. After the game, the stands emptied and rushed the field. It felt like something from a movie scene. It didn't dawn on me until I got home that God supernaturally healed my leg. I mean I just knew I tore my hamstring. This was my first time experiencing the healing power of God for myself. I mean I read about it in the Bible, but I didn't think it would actually happen for me.

This was one of the pivotal moments in my life that shifted my faith in God.

After that game, we lost the next round of playoffs at the Cowboy's stadium. Football was officially finished and I was heartbroken. I developed relationships with my teammates for the last four years and just like that, it was over. I felt like a regular Joe all over again. I finished up the school year running track and playing basketball. With the school year ending, signing day was around the corner. I always dreamed of putting on a LSU hat on signing day, but unfortunately my SAT scores were low so I had to go to junior college instead.

IT'S MUCH BIGGER

I started my first semester of college at Tyler Junior College (TJC) and I couldn't be more excited about it. TJC was about 3 hours from my home in Ft. Worth. I was excited about getting away from home because I felt like the black sheep of the family. Living with my dad, stepmom and two sisters, I always got the short end of the stick, being the only boy. Life at home for me was rough. I was treated differently from my other siblings. I had to do things that they were exempt from doing.

To be quite honest, I felt misunderstood and felt that I could not have an open conversation with my parents. Every time I would try to express how I feel, I would get shut down or dominated in a conversation. On the other hand, my sisters were able to freely express how they felt without getting shut down or punished. This caused me to be even more introverted and pulled me even deeper into isolation. There were times I would go in my room and not come out. I would sit and talk to God instead. I felt like He was the only one that understood me.

On my second day of school, after moving into my dorm room, we had our first football meeting. I was recruited to be a wide receiver, but instead I found myself in a position meeting with defensive backs. I walked into the room and I looked at the board and I saw that I was 6th on the depth chart. When I looked at it, I laughed on the inside. Like really? They got me 6th on the depth chart? Oh, I was furious.

I was always a person that let my skills speak for itself. My dad would always tell me "the cream always rises to the top." I knew it was only a matter of time before I got moved up in the depth chart. Two weeks had gone by since we started practicing and I felt like I was doing an amazing job. For some odd reason, my coaches were still keeping me at the bottom of the depth chart. I couldn't understand for the life of me why I was experiencing so much resistance. I wasn't used to being sidelined. I was always used to being the first choice and for the first time in my life that wasn't the case.

I remember going back to my dorm room questioning God about the situation. I didn't get any answers. I felt like He wasn't listening to me until one day, after the fourth game of the season, I heard a whisper "I'm trying to teach you patience."

You see as much as I felt that I was the best athlete on the team, God still wanted to teach me a lesson. This changed my perspective not only on football but life in general. At the time, I thought I was an extremely patient person but when you are faced with challenging situations that you have not been in before, it forces you to respond to that given situation. Mastering patience is one of the hardest things a person can go through. I feel like once you master patience, you can master anything. Sometimes "not yet" is the hardest response, especially when God says it. During this time, I can honestly say, it was the most humble I've ever been. Every day, I could hear God telling me, "Go lower."

Sometimes we feel like we've got it altogether, but more often than not, that's not the case. I went from being angry and upset to cheering my teammates on passionately. Every time I felt anger, bitterness or unforgiveness coming into my heart, I felt God telling me once again, "go lower."

Although I was doing everything God wanted me to do, things still didn't change. Not only did I feel that I should've been playing, but I was constantly reminded of that by my teammates. I was convinced that my coaches just didn't like me. I found myself being angry at God yet again. I remember repeatedly asking questions like "why are you telling me to do all these things if nothing is going to change?"

I went the entire season only getting a few plays a game. I swear it was like torture. I would always go back to my dorm room after the games and cry. I told my dad every week not to come to the games because I didn't want to waste his time if I wasn't going to play. One day while crying, I heard the Lord again speak to me in a small gentle voice and He said, "I've hidden you in plain sight. Yes you may be the most talented, but there's still more you need to learn."

I remember the immature response I gave Him. "God, why? It's just football."

He said, "no you're wrong, it is much bigger than football."

THE CALL

On a Thursday afternoon, after waking up from a long nap, I decided I was going to go to the library to do some extra studying to prepare for my upcoming exam. I dreaded being in my dorm room, it was always loud and full of distractions. While walking to the library, I was getting ready to cross the street and I heard the audible voice of God tell me, "I'm calling you into ministry and you will only play football for a season of your life."

I felt all the air leave my body. I stopped and started begging God, "please let me play longer."

I continued to the library to finish up my studies, but while in the library, I felt a strong unction to read my Bible. At the time, it had been a while since I read my Bible or attended church. I tried to ignore it for as long as I could, but it felt overwhelming. I decided I would leave the library and head back to my dorm room and read the Word. I pulled my Bible off the shelf and I did what most young Christians do, "God take me to the page that you want me to read."

I landed on Jeremiah 1:5 *"Before I formed you in the womb I knew you, before you were born I set you apart; I appointed you as a prophet to the nations."* After reading that Scripture, I felt the presence of God come upon me so strong in my dorm room. I felt it was a deeper meaning than just reading the Scripture. I felt like that Scripture was a part of my life, and a part of my DNA. At the time, I had no idea what a prophet was but God had led me to study the life of Jeremiah. It was something about his life and his ministry that was connected to mine.

It was the first time I was introduced to my identity in Jesus Christ. Things that didn't make sense in my life started to make sense. It was at this pivotal moment when things started to change in my life. My relationship with God started to grow and blossom. I started asking questions that I'd never asked before and I became more inquisitive about knowing who God really was. No longer did I have my parents there to push me, but I had to seek God on my own. It seems as if this is what he was waiting for all along. When I look back at it, God initiated the conversations until I started to initiate on my own.

He has a way of playing hide-and-seek. God often hides Himself so you can seek Him. Just like the Scripture says, "when you seek me with all of your heart, you will find me."

A few months went by, and spring ball was around the corner. I was excited and I felt like the time had come for my hard work to finally pay off. I was in the best shape of my life and I felt like I had a point to prove.

Two weeks into spring ball, I was killing it. You couldn't tell me anything. I was feeling like my old self again. I definitely had my swagger back. I was no longer Jonathan but my teammates started to call me "Hollywood." It was like showtime at the Apollo when I touched the field. Lights, camera, action baby!

After practice one day, the head coach from Abilene Christian University offered me an unofficial offer to his school. I didn't pay any mind to it, I had my eyes set on an SEC school. I didn't have any offers from them , but I knew it was only a matter of time before I did.

Later that afternoon, I headed back to my dorm room and I heard my teammates yelling and screaming across the hall. I decided to get up from my bed and see what the commotion was about. When I walked in the room, one of my teammates asked me if I heard the news.

"What news? I asked." "We are getting the Texas A&M quarterback, Matt Davis."

I went back to my room to see what all the hype was about. I went to YouTube to look at some footage and found out that he was a 5-star prospect coming out of high-school, so he was a pretty big deal. Two minutes into me watching his film, I could tell that he was a baller. This was just what we needed. I was smiling ear to ear, finally, I got a quarterback to throw me the ball. Later that week, after practice, the coach was finally introducing Matt to me and my teammates. After practice, everybody headed back to the dorm room and before I had a chance to make it to my dorm room, I saw Matt coming up the hall. We spoke briefly, I told him I was excited to have him as a teammate and I couldn't wait to get on the field to play together. Moments later, my coach called me and told me that I would have to change jersey number because Matt wanted number 4. I can't lie, I was pretty salty about that.

In the football world, the quarterbacks always get the first choice. I wanted to complain to the coaches, but I knew they weren't going to hear me out so I had to suck it up and take it as a loss. A few practices went by, we were getting ready for the season, and we found out that Matt was everything he was hyped up to be. I noticed he didn't talk much though and most players thought he was arrogant because he transferred from a bigger school. I thought otherwise. He seemed like a pretty cool dude to me. I decided to spend some time with him one day after class. I walked into his dorm room and to my surprise, there he was on the bed with his Bible opened.

I asked him, "whatchu' readin'?"

He responded, "the Bible."

I could tell he didn't want to be bothered but I was persistent. I was thinking to myself, "finally, somebody like me!" "You mind if I read with you," I asked.

"Yea sure, I don't mind. Pull up a chair."

A few minutes later, some of my teammates started sprinkling in one by one and before you know it, we were having a Bible study in our dorm room. An hour and a half had gone by and we were still having conversations about the Bible. When it was all said and done, Matt and I looked at each other and we were amazed as to what had just happened.

Word had gotten back to our coaches about what took place that night and we came up with a plan to start a football Bible study. We had Bible study two days a week! On Tuesdays and Thursdays. It didn't dawn on me until weeks later that this is what God was telling me all along. I didn't know that my season of going through various trials was preparing me to lead other young men. This is what God meant when He said, "it's bigger than football." Matt and my relationship grew stronger and stronger. Not only were we playing football, but we were leading young men to Christ. This was a big deal since a lot of the young men, including myself, had come from single-parent homes, some were fatherless, some were emotionally and physically abused and just like me, football was their way of escape. God used Matt and me as a bridge to connect them back to Him through the Bible study. For the first time in my life, I felt like I was living for my purpose outside of football.

After the first week of the next season, I was the leading receiver amongst all junior college athletes; then suddenly, things took a sharp turn. I was back at square one. I went from leading all receivers to being at the very bottom. I remember after the 5th game of the season, I decided I would talk to my coaches about it and to my surprise, the conversation didn't go anywhere. They didn't have any answers for me as to why I wasn't getting the ball like I should. I felt like football was being stripped from me. I was doing everything God asked me to do. I was doing better in school. I was staying away from parties. I wasn't smoking, doing drugs or any of that and I still felt like I was getting the short end of the stick.

While in the dorm room crying in a fetal position, I heard that voice again, "go lower." I didn't want to hear it. Why do I always have to go lower? God, why are you always requiring so much of me? Why do I have to go through all of this pain? When is it going to be my turn? When is it going to be my season? I remember asking God all of these questions and still no answer.

I decided I would cry harder, after all, this is what I learned in my church. If you danced a certain way or if you yelled loud enough, God would hear you, so I tried that and still no answer. I found out quickly that emotionalism doesn't work with God. I had to find another way. I dealt with this the entire football season. After the season came to a close, signing day was around the corner, and I still didn't have an offer from the schools that I wanted to go to. I had to sit and watch over 20 of my teammates sign their letter of intent to big name schools while I was left not signing to any school on signing day. You could only imagine how crushed I was to see everybody else getting promoted and I was getting overlooked. During this time, God wasn't saying anything to me. I couldn't hear His voice at all like I normally would. He would always give me that place of comfort every time I would go to Him, but for some reason during this time period, I didn't feel confident about God at all. I felt every emotion, every bit of pain, and every ounce of heartache, all of it.

BY HIS GRACE

Later, I got a phone call from the financial department informing me that I owed the school money for my room and board. I was furious because I didn't have any money to give them. I went to my coaches office to confront them about the situation.

I asked my coaches, "Can y'all explain why you took me off of scholarship?"

His response was "we were running low on scholarships for the new student athletes, so we had to take yours away."

"Couldn't y'all have told me anything? I could have prepared," I said.

They sat there with stone looks on their faces. I left my coach's office, and I tried to cry but I was out of tears. I decided to take matters into my own hands; I started reaching out to college coaches. When I got up and before I went to bed, I emailed and called college coaches. I would spend hours doing this every single day. Even though I was putting all the hard work in, I still wasn't getting the response that I wanted. One day while I was sending out emails, I got a knock on my dorm room and it was the head RA with a letter in his hand. He told me to read it immediately and when I read it, it said that I owed $2,000 for my room and board. I didn't know how I was going to come up with the money so I decided I would call my dad and ask if there was any way we could come up with $2000. When I called my dad, he gave me the "oh, I don't know what you're going to do. You're going to have to come home and work until you can come up with the money."

I tried not to take it personally, but my dad was very old school. It's not that he didn't love me, but he always taught me to work for what you want. Going back home and working was not the answer, so I told myself, "God you brought me here, so I expect you to take care of me while I'm here." I made up in my mind that I was staying until they kicked me out.

By the grace of God, I was able to go the entire semester without getting kicked out and they didn't say anything else to me after that day. I remember holding my breath every time I walked into the building trying to hide from the RA, hoping he didn't say anything to me. About two months later, school came to a close, and I was still stuck without a 4-year university to go to. Summer came quickly and I was still hammering away at the emails and phone calls until one day, I was working out in my friend's garage, and I got a call from Abilene Christian University saying they wanted to offer me a scholarship. After I hung up the phone with them, I felt the overwhelming presence of God come upon me again. It had been a while since I felt His presence. I wasn't talking to God for those few months because everything in my life was going downhill and I felt that He was partially responsible. After working out, I picked up my phone and I opened my Instagram account. When I opened my page, and I saw the first picture that I posted was my Tyler Junior College visit, I had an

Abilene Christian Football shirt on. I almost lost it. I was in a state of shock. Literally, God already had my school picked out for me. Although I felt like I was in control, God was in control the entire time. He had already ordered my steps.

A week later, my friends Dominique, Jaylen, and my dad headed up to Abilene Christian for a college visit. After meeting with the head coach, he informed me that he needed my official transcripts from Tyler Junior College to move forward in the recruiting process. While on the road, after leaving the school, I called TJC financial department and they informed me that I still owed $2000. I knew my dad didn't have the money so I didn't bother asking him. I prayed and tried to seek guidance as to what I should do, but I felt God tell me to rest and that He had everything under control.

Later that night, my uncle Bruce called me and said "hey, do you still owe that $2000 to your school? Get them on the line so I can pay it." My heart was beating through my chest. I was in a state of shock. God turned things around just that fast. I felt my confidence in God being restored again.

ABILENE

My 4-year college journey had finally arrived. ACU, here I come! I was excited about transitioning from Saginaw to Abilene, Texas. I heard a lot of negative things about Abilene. I heard Abilene was a small town with not much to do and just a dry place to be in with little activities. I could care less about those things. My mind was focused on playing football, getting my degree, and going to the NFL. Besides, I never did too much partying anyway and didn't plan on it. So if you ask me, it sounded like it was just the right place. After two and a half hours of driving, I made it to my on-campus apartment. My family and I unloaded my belongings and I signed my first apartment lease. I felt independent. What made it better, it was all paid for.

I remember like it was yesterday, it was scorching hot outside and if you are from the south, you know how Texas can get mid-July. After we finished unpacking, I said goodbye to my parents and I headed over to the football meeting room to get my equipment. I was really happy to be around my new teammates for the first time. We met for about two hours, introducing ourselves to one another and going over the expectations for the upcoming season. Shortly after, we broke off and went into position meetings. I walked in the room, I saw the depth chart on the screen, and I noticed I was at the very bottom. I sighed. Here we go again.

I instantly got upset about being last on the depth chart because the coaches had promised so much to me and told me that I would come in as a Junior and have the starting position but that was not the case. Although I was upset, I was used to being the underdog and I always constantly reminded myself that my play would speak for itself. This was something that my dad always told me and I continued to live by that. At that time, I could just hear my dad saying, "the cream always rises to the top, so don't worry about it, just go out there and play ball." I left that meeting and while walking back to my apartment, I was telling God all my frustrations and I heard Him say, "go lower."

It was at that moment that I realized that God didn't want to hear my excuses nor my complaints. It didn't matter what the coaches promised me prior to me coming to the school, He wanted me to handle the situation with humility and respond the way He always taught me to respond. Although I was in this situation before, I didn't pass the test. I believe that when tests fail, it is a test that you will have to take again. I felt God had put me in the situation purposely to see how I would respond to it. It was a moment where God was testing me to see if I would be a reflection of Him.

The following day I met up with my counselor to set up my class schedule. I originally planned on becoming an engineer but some of my classes from TJC didn't transfer, so I didn't meet the qualifications for the engineering program. Although I could've still got admitted into the program, I would've risked not playing football my first season. I always had a desire for creating and building things but my heart was in football.

Therefore, I ended up studying kinesiology with a focus on physical therapy. There was always something about the body that I loved. Being an athlete, I've had a lot of injuries in my past and I've always been thrilled to learn how the body recovers and how to use proper mechanics to prevent further injuries. I finally got all of my classes squared away. With ACU being a Christian University, we were all forced to take Bible classes. I noticed throughout the first couple weeks of taking classes that my devotional time with God had significantly decreased. Studying the Bible and spending time with God started to feel like a chore. I mean between going to school chapel, going to the football chapel and having old testament & new testament assignments, it was weighing on me. I still felt a tug to start a football Bible study, but I didn't want to overload myself and others, so I ignored the voice of God.

One day I was in the cafeteria and I met a man by the name of Ryan Bowman who later became one of my biggest mentors. We connected instantaneously. Mr. Bowman was in his mid-30s but he had a fiery passion for helping young African American men like me become something of themselves. Ever since I was a child, I've always been attracted to having conversations with older people. I remember when I was a toddler, I used to sit outside under the tree, in front of my grandmother's house, and listen to her talk all day while my brother was out in the neighborhood with our friends. I found myself spending time with Mr. Bowman just like I did with my grandmother. He would give me tools on how to navigate through life mentally, physically, and spiritually. He was a key cog in my success during my time at ACU.

TURNED TABLES

Practice after practice, I was still stuck in the same spot. Not that I wasn't talented enough, but it was because my coaches wanted the seniors to start the season. It was not necessarily based upon how well you could perform so I had to wait for my opportunity. Week 1 arrived, and we were hours away from our first game against Georgia State in Atlanta at the Mercedes Benz stadium.

My coaches had promised me that I would get a lot of playing time in this game. I called my family members, my friends, everybody back home and told them to watch the game. It was a nationally televised game, because it was the first game of the season. We arrived at the stadium, I walked in the locker and laid all my equipment out. I wanted to be the flyest person on the field. You know the motto, "when you look good you feel good, and when you feel good, you play good." Kick off was moments away and an ESPN news reporter pulled me to the side and wanted to interview me before the game. At this point, the pressure was on and it was time to perform. The game finally started and I stood by my coach anxiously waiting to get into the game.

The first quarter went by and my coach still didn't put me in the game. The second quarter went by, and I was still on the sideline. I went back into the locker room during halftime, texted my dad and told him, "just wait, I'm going to get in sooner or later."

The third quarter was on the way, and I started stretching, warming up because I felt my number would get called at any moment. Moments later my teammate pulled me to the side and told me "they are not going to put you in the game." I was upset, but the reality of me getting in the game went away. Honestly, I had a gut feeling I wasn't going to play, but I didn't want to let my family and friends down (from back home) after getting them all excited about watching me play.

A few more weeks of the season went by and I was still only getting little playing time until the 4th week of the season when my defensive coach pulled me to the side and asked me if I could still play defensive back.

I told him yes. "C'mon coach you know I can."

"Okay son, you're my guy, don't let me down," he responded. It was a day before the game when he told me I would be starting but I had confidence I could get the job done. This was my moment to not only show my teammates but my coaches that I deserve to play. We had a big match up against Central Arkansas and we were big underdogs. I called my family and told them we were playing in Dallas not too far from home. Gameday arrived and I was really excited for my first season start. Kick off was on the way, my family and Dominique were in the stands cheering me on. That was all the support I needed. I had one of the best games of my college career. Even with a short week of practice, I still went out and accomplished everything I set out to do. I was even nominated conference player of the week. The tables were finally turning in my favor. I finally passed the test after so much trial and error. I felt like God was proud of the way I handled the adversity. He put me in.

Sometimes, God hides you in plain sight until it's your time to blossom. It's not that you're not good enough or smart enough. It is just that God has appointed time for you to flourish. This game changed the course of my college career.

Outside of football, I didn't do much at ACU. I was always in my room, watching films or watching movies in my apartment. My teammates begged me to go out but I refused, until one time they were able to convince me to go out to the club. While in the club that night, I was standing next to two Latino men and they started arguing. Before you know it, one of them pulled out a knife and stabbed the other. I witnessed it three feet away from me!

This ruined my clubbing experience while in college. I took it as a sign that the club wasn't a place I was supposed to be. When I got back to my apartment that night, I opened my Bible. I hadn't read my Bible for the past three months. While reading, I could feel God telling me, "why haven't you started a Bible study?" He had been reminding me to start it since the first week of school my junior year, but again like I stated previously, going to a Christian school where you *have to* take Bible classes and attend chapel every day of the week becomes monotonous. Reading my bible felt like a job at times. Even while attending chapel, it didn't feel genuine, but instead felt *religious.*

THE STRUGGLE

Throughout the semester, I was still battling my pornography addiction. It became worse over the years, and it was secretly damaging almost every area of my life. From high school, to TJC and now Abilene, my addiction grew. I tried to stop on my own, but I just couldn't. I tried to will my way through it and it didn't work. I tried to watch self-help videos but that didn't work either. At this point, I felt like I would never get free from pornography. In my head, I knew it was wrong, but something inside of me was controlling me.

Romans 7:15 was more real to me than ever when Paul states I do not understand what I do. For what I want to do I do not do, but what I hate I do." Sometimes you don't understand until you have experienced it. Even certain scriptures don't come alive to you until you have tasted that same experience.

As my football season continued, I got more playing time each game. I went from not playing at all to starting on offense, defense, and returning kicks on special teams. There were only a few players in all of college football that could do this, and I was one of them. I got to experience what most players didn't throughout my career, I got to experience every part of the game week in and week out. I remember after every game needing to be helped to the locker room due to exhaustion.

Funny that I was complaining about not getting the opportunity to play but now feeling like I was playing too much. I guess it's true when people say, "be careful what you ask for because you just might get it." Although things were turning around for me in regard to football, I was still fighting an internal battle with myself about my mother not being there.

Even with all the success that I was getting, it was still my heart's desire to see my mother in the stands. I always imagined taking her the winning game ball after a game. After a while, I felt like it was just a fantasy of mine and it would never come true.

The rest of my junior year was robotic. It consisted of going to class, working out, studying film, and hanging out in my apartment watching

Game of Thrones. There was one exception though, which was the highlight of my spring semester. I would hang out with Mr. Bowman on Sundays.

He would pick me up to go to church. We would drive out to the country to the church where he preached. The church was small and most of the congregation were elderly. I remember my first time visiting, I was overwhelmed with joy. The people were so kind and loving. They treated me like I was one of their own. We would all hang out after church and eat a home cooked meal. The food was delicious, and I was always left with the 'itis'. There's a saying in the African-American community, "if you don't have the 'itis' after you eat, then the food wasn't good." Trust me, that was not the case. Between the hot water cornbread, homemade mac n' cheese, greens, and black eye peas, it always left me slumped.

I finished up the rest of my semester strong in my classes. I wanted to get ahead of schedule and graduate early after my senior season. I wanted to prepare for the NFL draft without worrying about finishing my college degree.

RUNNING ON FUMES

With summer approaching, my uncle Bruce called me and asked me if I wanted to come to Virginia to train for my senior year. I hesitated for a moment, but I knew it would be good for me to get out of Texas and get a breath of fresh air. I agreed to fly up there and train with him for the summer. About a week later, I flew to Virginia and my uncle and I began training. It was one of the best experiences of my life. My uncle is just a few years older than me, but he has always been one of my biggest role models. I think it is important for every male to have another strong male role model in their life. Day in and day out, we would workout, watch film and hangout. I don't remember paying for anything. My uncle took care of all my expenses.

I would sit and think at times, "why am I closer to my mother's brother than I am her?" my uncle would always ask me, "have you talked to your mother?" I knew that this was his way of trying to get us to communicate, but at this point, my heart was hardened toward my mother. I didn't want anything to do with her. I could care less whether we talked or not. This was my new norm. While I was in Virginia, I started dating one of my track teammates from ACU. We would talk every day after my workout. She was athletic, smart, ambitious and older than me. I was still into older women, and she fit the mold of what I wanted.

After summer ended, I flew back to Abillene Christian two days before training camp. I was in tip top shape and was ready for the season. The only thing that was on my mind was finishing out my senior year and making it to the NFL. Every day, that was all I thought about. Whether I was in class, at practice, at home, studying, or even while hanging out with my friends, all I could think about was going pro. At this point, it was football or nothing. I can honestly say I thought about football more than I thought about God. It was the first thing that was on my mind every morning and my obsession grew stronger every day. I took a few summer classes so I was still on track to graduate early. At this point, getting my degree wasn't as important to me as it was in the past. I decided I would take a few hours less than I originally planned, so that I could focus more on my senior season. The season finally started and we played our first game at Fresno State. As expected, I had an amazing game, and the momentum carried through most of my senior season. I noticed I didn't get to enjoy most of the games though because I wasn't present. My mind was always on the future. Every week that went by, I felt more and more empty. I was paralyzed with fear of not making it to the NFL.

There were moments where I would literally have anxiety attacks before games, and no one knew it. My girlfriend and I were getting close, but I still didn't feel comfortable talking to her about it. Actually, I didn't talk to anyone about it. One day I finally decided I would talk to Mr. Bowman about what was going on. After class I stopped by his office, and we had a conversation about all that was happening. I felt if I didn't talk to somebody about it, I would go crazy. After all I was wondering, am I the only person that thinks like this? I needed answers and I felt like Mr. Bowman was the man to talk to. He told me that I had a bright future and not to be so obsessed with football. He told me that I should always have a plan B and never put all my eggs in one basket. To be quite honest, that's not the answer I was looking for. I continued the season playing but I felt empty still. I didn't find any joy in playing anymore. I was always battling a voice of fear in my mind and I didn't know how to overcome it. I ended my senior season emptier than I'd ever been.

SOUL TIES

My mindset affected all areas of my life. I was doing terrible in all of my classes and my relationship was taking a turn for the worst. When we first started dating, we enjoyed each other's company. We had a lot of common interests. We were both star athletes. Both of us were very ambitious and we enjoyed having fun. With her being a year older than me, she taught me a lot of things. I would often get side tracked with chasing football and my grades were slipping. She would always make sure I kept my goals in check. She ran track and field professionally for Trinidad & Tobago. She gave me a lot of pointers on how to carry myself as a professional athlete. We spent countless hours studying, working out and enjoying each other's company.

Somewhere along the way, I decided that I didn't want to have sex anymore. She was furious about it. I thought I was doing us both a favor by trying to do the right thing and stop having sex. It seemed like that was the driving force of our relationship. To be quite honest, I knew I was disappointing God the entire time but I didn't want to upset her, so I just kept doing it.

Eventually I decided I would take a stand and do things God's way. After I made the decision to do that, I could tell that she didn't want any parts of the relationship anymore. It was probably best for us to separate but the soul tie was so strong that I didn't have the strength to do it, therefore I stayed in the relationship. Although, in my mind, I left a long time ago. Besides, my biggest weakness has always been my heart. I hate seeing people hurting especially when I feel like I am the cause of it. I was more sexually active than I'd ever been. I found myself trying to use sex as an escape from my issues. I started to realize that my relationship with her was just built on lust.

I knew God was telling me to leave the relationship months prior because He didn't ordain it. I often found myself trying to bargain with God like most of us do. I thought maybe if I would bring God into our relationship then things would change. I started reading the Bible to her a couple days throughout the week and it seemed like she was all for it. I could tell that I wanted it more for her than she did for herself. In my mind, I thought I could turn her into the woman I wanted her to be and God would approve of it. This is probably one of the worst mistakes of my life.

I learned that when God hasn't ordained a relationship, you shouldn't force yourself to stay in that relationship. If God says no, you should never say yes. Every day, I started distancing myself more and more. She would ask questions like; where have you been? Why are you acting so different? I would always give nonchalant answers like; I was working out or studying for my exam. I was just buying myself time until I had the strength to leave the relationship.

SHATTERED

The rest of my fall semester of my senior year I found myself playing catch up with most of my classes. I was in the library almost every day doing extra credit assignments to bring my grades up. I told myself I wouldn't be that athlete that would wait last minute to do things but sadly I did just that. Between juggling football, practice, film study, homework and maintaining my relationship, it was a handful.

During this time, I also started my preparation for the NFL draft. I ended both my junior and senior year with All American honors at three different positions. I was the first in school history to do so. I started receiving a lot of interest from different agencies that wanted to represent me. I felt like all the hard work from the past four years was about to pay off. My dreams were right there in front of my face and it seemed like nothing could stop me from achieving them.

I trained at a nearby facility with a few other teammates. A month and a half into training, I received a workout for the Houston Texans. While working out 3 days prior to my visit, I sprained my ankle. My ankle was the size of a baseball. I was still determined to go and workout anyway. This was an opportunity of a lifetime and I didn't want to let it pass me by. My agent suggested that I did not go, but I went anyway. Nothing, I mean nothing was going to get in the way of me doing what I needed to do. While at the workout, I was in extreme pain but my pride wouldn't let me quit. After the workout, the results were on the internet. I didn't run so well because of my ankle injury but I was still one of the top performers out of the entire workout. I knew for sure it was only a matter of time until I got a call. I headed over to Matt's house afterwards since he didn't stay too far from the NRG stadium. When I got to his house, before getting in the shower, I leaned over to take the bandage off of my ankle and I heard the Holy Spirit say, "you're not going to need an agent." I thought to myself how absurd is that? Every athlete has an agent that represents them. Shortly after, I drove back up to Abilene to finish my final exams and train. Pro day finally came around and it was time to perform. Dominique called me early that morning to let me know he was driving up to come and support me. I talked to my dad briefly that morning but none of my family could make it.

Nobody came to support me but Dominique.

Although this was a big day for me and I would have liked for them to be there, I didn't have time to have a pity party. It was business as usual. Later that afternoon, I arrived at school and shortly after I started preparing for my first workout. I was extremely nervous. I normally didn't get nervous before big games but I had put so much pressure on myself, I couldn't help but feel the pressure of the moment. In the blink of an eye, my pro day was over. I put up all the numbers statistically that I wanted to.

Now it was just a waiting game.

The day I had been waiting for was finally here. My dad threw me a party and my friends and family sat around the living room TV excited for my name to pop up on the screen. I knew I wasn't going to get picked up the first five rounds but there was a strong possibility I would hear my name in the later rounds. One round after another went by and we were still staring at the TV. The last few picks were slowly approaching and my name still wasn't called. My heart was sinking in my chest. I was so embarrassed and disappointed. My agent and I hadn't talked all day. He was nowhere to be found. The draft ended and I was still staring at the TV, daydreaming. My dad asked me if I wanted something to eat. I could tell he knew I was upset but I was too heartbroken to talk about it. I decided I would escape to the front yard and talk to God about it. I laid in the grass, looked up at the sky, and asked God "why is this happening to me? Why am I going through this? If you knew this was going to happen, why didn't you tell me? While I was talking to God, Dominique came outside to check on me. He asked me if I was okay. I tried to keep it together but I busted out in tears. I was crying uncontrollably. I felt overwhelmed with emotions.

Life without football wasn't a life that I wanted to live.

At about 3 a.m., I decided that I would drive up to my high school stadium. This is often where I would come and talk to God. I felt that God would always meet me there and this is where I could hear His voice the clearest. Whenever I felt sad, depressed or angry, this was my place of comfort. I would always remember Him telling me to pick up my football and play with it like I did as a child in my bedroom.

At this moment, my heart was heavy. I was filled with a ton of emotions. I started asking God why everything was unfolding the way it was. Football was the only thing that I had. It was my escape from my issues. It was the only thing that gave me comfort. Now this was gone too, and I couldn't wrap my mind around it. My mother left me at 5, I moved states due to Hurricane Katrina, I lost my grandmother, and my brother was locked up in prison. Football was the only thing that helped me cope with the losses in my life and now that was taken away too. Football was the canvas I would use to paint my emotions and express myself.

I remember that long heartfelt prayer and it seemed as if God wasn't even listening to me. I didn't feel any comfort from Him at all so I decided I would try crying harder and still nothing. I felt abandoned, alone, and depressed. I found out emotionalism was not the answer.

IT'S A WRAP

A few days later, I went back to Abilene to finish the rest of the school year. My girlfriend was getting ready to head back to Trinidad & Tobago for Olympic trials. We got into a really heated argument about her leaving. Her visa was expiring and she wanted me to marry her before she left. God knows I had love for her and didn't want her to miss out on an opportunity of a lifetime to compete in the Olympics, because she wanted to stay behind with me. I was finally able to convince her to leave. Her family gave me a really hard time about it. Marriage was the last thing on my mind. I had other things to worry about. Besides, I didn't have a job, a house, or a career. Graduation was around the corner and I was still scrambling to get some last minute assignments done. By the grace of God, I found favor with most of my professors and was able to get everything done before graduation. This time around, I didn't owe the school any money. My room and board was taken care of, my last class was paid off and I was even offered an on campus job working the spring games.

While working one of the spring games, I called my agent and fired him. We hadn't spoken in weeks, he was always giving me the run around saying he was talking to this team and that team but I knew it was a lie. Afterall, I remember God telling me that I wasn't going to need an agent and thought maybe that was the cause of me being delayed. I mean at this point, I didn't have anything to lose. So why not do it God's way?

I knew the next thing he wanted me to do was breakup with my girlfriend, but I knew I would need a lot more convincing. Graduation finally came around and a few of my family and friends came into town to watch me walk the stage. I could remember the look on my dad's face. He was extremely proud. I was one of the first to graduate from college on my dad's side of the family, so this was a pretty big deal. I was happy God used me to break a generational curse off of my family. I remember walking across the stage jumping for joy. I felt like I graduated for me and my brother. As much as I tried to downplay getting my degree, it was a big deal when I look back at it. My dad was big on my siblings and I graduating from college because he didn't have the opportunity to finish.

Football wasn't going the way we had expected but graduating from college was something I could use to make my dad proud of me. I stayed in Abilene for another two weeks. I wasn't excited to go back home. I enjoyed my independence, and I knew when I got back home, all of that would go out of the window. The morning before I left Abilene, I went out to the lake in my apartments and spent some time with God thanking Him for all that He had done over the past two years while being at ACU. It was a once in a lifetime experience that I would never forget. Dominique and I packed everything up and headed back to Ft. Worth that afternoon. My college career had ended and I was heading home. It was at that moment that I realized my life was going to change forever.

SAGINAW

I'm back home in Saginaw and it feels like I took 10 steps backwards. I got my college degree but I still felt empty inside. I thought to myself, "why do people put so much emphasis on obtaining a college degree?"

Most people that get a degree don't pursue a career in the field that they study. I believe that education is important and my father instilled that in me at a young age, but if you don't love what you're doing, it's like dying a slow death. Every day you will wake up asking yourself, "what if I would've done what I truly wanted to do in life?"

I wasn't willing to take that risk so I continued to pursue my dreams of playing football. I hardly had any money, and I needed to pay for my training. My parents were also on me every day about coming up with a plan so that I could contribute to some of the bills. A week later after applying for several jobs, I landed a part-time Job with Amazon distribution center as a packer. Every day I would go to work. I hated every minute of it. It felt like it was a hundred degrees in the warehouse, and we only got a 10-minute break during our shift. I tried to make the best of it, but it didn't last very long. I always enjoyed making everyone laugh, and tried to make the best out of my current situation. I lasted about two months before I quit, but I knew I had to find another Gig soon or else I wasn't going to hear the end of it from my parents.

Dominique and I continued to train every day, and I continued to market myself to as many professional teams as I could. I didn't bother looking for another agent, because I knew God specifically told me not to. Later that week I got a call From BC Lions of the Canadian Football League. They had an upcoming workout in three weeks, and they wanted me to attend. After I got the call, I confirmed that I would go to the tryout. Dominique and I started prepping for the workout and about two weeks out while during sprints, I pulled my hamstring. I thought to myself, "here we go again." It felt like every time I was about to walk through a door it was getting closed in my face. I felt like I had an opportunity of a lifetime and didn't want to withdraw from the workout. I started rehabbing with my high school trainer to get me back up to speed, but I knew I wasn't going to be 100%. Even if I had to workout on one leg, I was willing to do that rather than throwing in the towel. The workout was finally here and I still wasn't feeling like myself. I took about 5 ibuprofens before I worked out so that I wouldn't feel the pain. During the workout, I did exceptionally well. I was able to manage the pain and get through the workout. I just knew that a phone call was coming soon. Later that night, the team reached out to me, said they would get back to me, and they loved what they saw. I just knew this was my big break.

A couple days went by and I hadn't heard anything back from them. I decided to follow up but I got no response. At this point, my dad was considering that I should move on from football. His logic was that I had a 4-year degree that should be used. I had no intentions on hanging up the cleats until God told me otherwise. I still had a burning passion to finish what I started and I wasn't willing to let anyone stop me, not even my parents. I felt as if God was telling me to continue but my parents were telling me to go in a different direction. I was so conflicted because I felt I was going in the direction that he wanted me to, but the doors kept closing. I began to question whether I was hearing from God or not and perhaps maybe my parents were right and it was time for me to move on.

I started applying for other jobs and landed another job with another distribution center. I worked overnight in a refrigerated warehouse that was about 12 degrees. I didn't like working there but I felt like it was the only option I had. By this time, my confidence was at an all time low and I wanted to just go and hide myself. I knew I could've made a quick phone call and got a coaching job with my high school but I was filled with pride, shame and self-condemnation. I didn't want to answer all the questions on why I didn't make it, so I decided I would hide instead. I never cried so much in my life. I would go in my room and sleep all day until it was time for me to go to work or workout. I didn't want to deal with the realities that life was throwing at me so I thought sleeping would help me avoid them. My girlfriend and I were still seeing each other but she was back home in Trinidad & Tobago. She had just made it to the Olympic Trials and I was home working a "nine-to-five."

I felt like a nobody. I felt like everyone was excelling except me. My life was quicksand. It was like I was stuck and there was nothing I could do about it. The tension between my parents and me grew. They felt like I was wasting time but I was just buying myself time until I got a phone call. They decided to add more to my responsibilities so they stopped paying for my phone bill and wanted me to pay an additional bill towards the house for living there. In their eyes, they thought it was time for me to take on more since I graduated. To be quite honest, I didn't feel like it was my house anymore, I felt like a guest.

After a while, I decided I would give God another week for an opportunity to come and if it didn't, I would change careers. One afternoon, during the summer, Dominique and I went to go workout at the nearby high school. While working out, I received a phone call from a

Canadian phone number. I didn't answer because I didn't know who it was. After the workout, before leaving the field, I noticed a voicemail on my phone. I listened to the voicemail and it was the general manager for the Toronto Argonauts. He was wondering if I had my passport because he wanted to fly me out for an official workout. After listening, I was startled because I just planned to throw in the towel. I didn't have an agent because I fired him and there wasn't anybody to market me to their organization. I was walking off the field and I heard God tell me that He had everything under control. I heard Him tell me that all he wanted me to do was rest.

Oftentimes, the world tells us to work, but God wants us to rest so He can work for us. I thought that I could will my way through to success without God. When I got to the place where I could let go, God opened the door. Three days went by and I flew to Toronto to workout. They took care of all my expenses and gave me money while I was there. I thought to myself, "if this is what being in the pro's feels like, I'm here for it." I didn't get to tour the city much, but from what I saw, it was beautiful.

Later the next day, I had my one on one workout with the staff. I had an amazing workout and they told me they would be in contact with me before they offer a contract. While on the flight back home, I was happier than I had ever been in a long time. Things started to make sense and my views on waiting started to change.

When I made it home, my parents were inquiring about the workout. I can't lie, I was pretty bitter about it. I thought they were asking just to ask; I wondered if they truly cared. I'm sure they did, just not as much as I did. Even though the workout went well, I still didn't have a contract. A couple weeks went by and I still didn't hear anything back from Toronto. I asked God, "why send me up there if you're going to put me through this again?"

I was angry at God and decided I would do what I always did to get a release. When I got back home to my room, after taking a long walk. I reached under my bed, grabbed a bottle of lotion, and I started watching pornography. This time in the middle of watching it, I felt something different than I normally did. I couldn't put my finger on it but it was as if something overcame me. After I finished watching a few videos, I fell asleep. A few hours later, I tried to wake up and I couldn't. I felt someone on top of me, holding me down. I fought for about 10 minutes trying to wake up, but I couldn't. There is no other way to describe it other than terrifying. I couldn't open my eyes as much as I wanted to. I couldn't move my arms or even my legs, I felt paralyzed and hopeless. The only thing I could think of was Jesus, and when I said His name (in my mind), whatever was holding me down, let me go.

I woke up, and got out of bed panicking. I opened my closest door, I looked under my bed and I opened my room door to see if anyone was in my room. No one was there. I thought to myself I know I'm not going insane. It felt so real, and I knew I wasn't losing my mind. My heart was still beating a hundred miles an hour, and I didn't know what to do.

I opened my Bible and I heard God tell me to go on a seven day fast by myself. I never fasted before outside of a corporate fast, but I knew this is what God was leading me to do. I was always hesitant to do things I didn't fully understand, but after that experience, it made me obey God quickly.

THE AWAKENING

While on my seven day fast I had many dreams and visions that changed my life completely. It was like the scales were removed from my eyes and I was seeing with a new set of eyes. The first night of my fast I had my first night vision. In the vision I was staring at myself laying in my bed, and beside me was a demonic figure laying next to me. As I looked closer I noticed we were chained up together. I noticed I was bound to him and he was bound to me. I then began feeding the demon, and as I fed him he grew bigger and bigger until he became a giant.

I asked God, "why are you showing me this?"

He responded by saying, "this is what's happening to you every time you watch pornography. This is the demon you have been feeding for the past 10 years."

I asked Him, "how did it grow into a giant?"

"It grew because you keep feeding it when you watch pornography. It has now become a stronghold in your life."

I asked God, "how do I get free from the bondage I was currently in?"

"Son stop feeding it"

I woke up moments later in a cold sweat. I had dreams in my past, but nothing as real as this. I was afraid to go back to sleep, because I didn't want to have another dream like that one. Growing up I have never heard of such things before, and I don't know anybody that shared in the experience I had. I opened up my bible and read aloud to comfort myself.

While reading I felt God telling me to log the dream in a book, because there were more to come. As I was writing, the Holy Spirit began to give me wisdom, revelation, and interpretation to my dream. I titled the dream *How to slay a Giant.* If a giant eats what you feed them, then you must learn to stop feeding them or else they will continue to grow in your life. Giants, which are representatives of demonic strongholds, don't break overnight. You must learn to pray and fast to weaken it.

I was ignorant to the fact that I was fighting a spiritual battle. I had read the scripture many times that "We wrestle not against flesh and blood". I didn't understand the magnitude of that particular scripture, because it had not become a reality to me. The enemy used my ignorance as a tool against me. I tried many ways to get free: self-help books, videos, and I even tried keeping a tally of streaks on my quest to sobriety. None of those worked for me. It's not that I wasn't fighting to get free, I was just fighting wrong.

The bible declares in Ephesians 6:12, "for we wrestle not against flesh and blood but against principalities, against powers, against the rulers of darkness of this world, and against spiritual wickedness in high places." This is where my deliverance process began right at home in my bedroom. I learned that everything is spiritual. Whatever happens in the spirit manifests itself in the natural. I learned that dreams and vision are one of the many tools that God uses to communicate. It is God's way of informing us of what is taking place in the spirit realm. I learned that there is nothing hidden in the spirit. I often watched pornography at night, because I thought no one could see me. After having this encounter, I found out that wasn't the case. Whatever you do in the dark, it will come to the light.

Paul wrote in 2nd Corinthians 2:11 "Lest Satan should get an advantage for we are not ignorant of his devices." In the scripture, Paul was letting us know that the enemy uses sin as a device to keep us snared. For example, imagine taking a tracking device and placing it inside of someone's phone, wherever that person goes, you can track their every move, because the tracking device is a part of the phone. What happens if the person doesn't know the tracking device is there? How will they know to get rid of it? The only way to get rid of it is to recognize that there is a tracking device inside of your phone and separate your phone from the tracking device. Pornography was a device the enemy was using to destroy my life but I was ignorant of the fact; not knowing that I was being tracked and attacked.

God gave me the opportunity to free myself from this bondage I was in for the past 10 years. Jesus told His disciples in Matthew 17:21, "but this kind does not go out except by praying and fasting." They were struggling to cast out demons and Jesus corrected them by letting them know that there are certain kinds of spirits that are only casted out by way of fasting and praying. It had been over 10 years living with a pornography addiction so you can only imagine how big the stronghold was in my life. I had to fast to weaken its grip on my life. Although I had instructions on how to set myself free, I still had to choose to do right or wrong on a daily basis. Throughout my deliverance process, the knocking persisted, but God gave me strength to not open that door in my life. It didn't just happen overnight, I had to yield to the Holy spirit and follow his blueprint to my freedom. I had to choose to starve myself of something I repeatedly did for the past 10 years.

There's so much you can learn when you study the *Art of War*. For example, during WWII, the Germans blockaded western allies' railroad and canal access to stop shipment of food and supplies. Their strategy was to starve out their enemy. They knew if they achieved this, it didn't matter how big or dangerous their enemy was, they would eventually self-destruct.

Look at it this way, the enemy needs a doorway to enter your life, but when all the doors are shut there is no way it can enter in. The enemy has no strength in your life, except the strength you give it. The giant only grows if you feed it. Always remember, if there is no enemy within then the enemy outside can do you no harm.

I woke up the next morning still perplexed about what all happened that night. I was led to read the book of Matthew. Matthew has always been one of my favorite books of the Bible. I love learning about the kingdom of God and how it works. In the book of Matthew, I was able to study the life of Jesus and His purpose and plan for His kingdom. As a child, I grew up in the church and I was always inquisitive to know more about God but didn't know how to get there outside of church sermons.

At this moment in my life, my hunger and thirst for God grew even more. No matter how far I began to sink, God continuously reeled me back in. As I read and studied the scriptures for hours, more revelations started to come than I'd ever received before. It was like the words were popping off the pages, especially the words written in red when Jesus spoke. One thing that always stood out to me was that Jesus was with His disciples for many years and yet He was still a mystery to them. Another thing that stood out is how eloquently He spoke and the way He used parables to convey spiritual truths to the minds of unbelievers.

When His disciples asked Jesus why He speaks in parables, His response was, "You've been given the intimate experience of insight into the hidden mysteries of the realm of heaven's kingdom, but they have not. For everyone who listens with an open heart will receive progressively more revelation until he has more than enough. But those who don't listen with an open, teachable heart, even the understanding that they think they have will be taken from them. That's why I teach the people using parables, because they think they are looking for truth, yet because their hearts are unteachable, they never discover it" (Matthew 13:11-13 TPT).

As I dug deeper into the scripture. Jesus had many run-ins with the Pharisees and Sadducees. They were experts of the Law; they knew all of the Levitical laws, commandments, and teachings of Moses. All the aspects of religion, they knew it. What they failed to understand was that the One Moses and the prophets wrote about was standing right in the midst of them. They denied His authenticity as the Messiah and Jesus was a stranger to them.

I grew up in a religious setting. Jesus was a stranger to me. I knew all the practices and formalities of church. I knew the moral right things and wrong things to do. I knew everything but Jesus.

College dug deeper into that hole of religion. I was in an institution where they didn't even believe in using instruments during chapel, and had their own particular ways of doing things. I often wondered where Jesus was in all of this and was any of it biblical. I grew up in a church where if you wanted God to do something you had to run, shout, and dance until you passed out. I was in an environment where rules mattered more than relationship. Simply missing church was viewed as committing a sin. I grew up Baptist and later found out there were 100s of denominations. I always wondered why? There is only one Jesus and one gospel.

Sadly I was in church every Sunday but I was still bound to pornography. Learning about wealth and prosperity didn't help me with my addiction nor did I know that my addiction was spiritual. I knew all the scriptures, but just like the pharisees I was blinded by religion. (I had no true relationship with Jesus).

THE COURTROOM

I went the rest of the day isolating myself from my family and friends and just focusing on my fast. I checked my email periodically to see if any teams had reached out to me and if Toronto sent me a contract that was recently promised. I didn't want to consume myself too much with it and get distracted from my fast. Besides, football was the last thing on my mind after experiencing that dream the night before. There were still parts of me that felt like I was losing it. I decided to phone a friend and tell him about it, but before I picked up the phone to call, I felt God telling me not to say anything until He permitted me to.

Before you knew it, it was 10 p.m. and I was off to bed. Little did I know that I was about to have one of the most impactful encounters with God of my life. I entered into a vision that night. I saw a man standing outside of a royal gate that was connected to a royal kingdom. He had on a white robe with a red cross on the back of it that looked to be marked in blood. I could tell he was a watchman of some sort, and that he was on guard. Across from him, a few miles away, I saw another kingdom. It was full of darkness and there was a demonic figure pacing back and forth in front of it. I could feel the rage and anger in its heart, and his hatred for the man that was standing outside of the other gate. Immediately, my eyes were focused on the man that I previously saw standing outside the gate with a red cross on his back. I noticed something different this time. There was a dagger lodged inside of his ribcage and it was giving off a sense of light. For some odd reason, he didn't know the dagger was there and I thought to myself, "why can't he feel it?" It seemed like it was there for a while and he learned how to live with it.

Not only did I see the dagger, but the light illuminating from it caught the eye of the demonic figure that was standing in front of the other gate.

After the demonic figure saw it, he reported what he saw to a man dressed in all black. The man then began to walk towards the other gatekeeper with a briefcase in his hand. When he approached him, he walked right past him as if he didn't even exist. I then noticed that there was a meeting being held inside of the royal kingdom and they were strategizing for war against the kingdom of darkness. After the man in the black suit entered the royal gates, he came through the back door where the meeting was being held, unnoticed. He listened to all the plans that were being shared and after the meeting was adjourned, he left and reported back to his kingdom. While on the way back, I saw other demonic figures accompanying him. They were on horses and the man in the black suit began to hand over deeds that were in his hand and he gave them instructions to go and conquer different regions of the royal kingdom. All of a sudden, I was standing in a courtroom. The courtroom appeared to be a normal looking courtroom like here on earth.

While I was in that courtroom, my attorney and I, who was dressed in all white were facing the judge. The man in the black suit was present and he stood to the left of us. I didn't know what was going on initially, but I quickly found out that I was on trial. The man in the black suit began to open the briefcase that he was previously carrying. When he opened that briefcase, he pulled out a long scroll with my name on it, and it had over thousands of sins that I had committed during my life on earth. Suddenly, he began to call out the things that were written on the scroll. I literally felt my heart sink to my stomach, because I was guilty of all of the accusations that were being brought before me. I was terrified, and I didn't have the strength to utter a word. There was nothing that I could've said or tried to use to cover up what I had already done. Everything had already been recorded the moment it happened.

Momentarily my focus shifted to my attorney standing next to me. At this point I figured all hope was lost. As I gazed in his direction I noticed that my attorney, dressed in white, had a briefcase in His hand. He then proceeded to open up the briefcase and when He opened it up, He pulled out a scroll of his own that was identical to the scroll that the man in black presented. When He opened it up, I saw my name on the top of it, and it had all of the accusations that the previous scroll had. I thought to myself, "well I'm guilty at this point and there is no way around it."

As my attorney started to read off all the sins I had committed, I noticed something very different about the bottom of the scroll. My focus was immediately drawn to it. At the bottom of the scroll appeared fresh drops of blood that covered the rest of the scroll. The verdict read *Not guilty.*

I woke up feeling an overwhelming sense of peace that I have never felt before in my life. It was an eternal state of peace. I felt as light as a feather. My journal which I decided would be my dream book was right next to me in my bed. I reached over, turned my night light on and began to log my encounter. Not only was pornography ruining my life, but condemnation was destroying me too. For the first time in months, I felt free. I began to write until I couldn't write anymore. The revelation from my encounter started to pour out of me. The Holy Spirit led me as I wrote and gave me the interpretation of what I had just experienced in my encounter.

The watchman that was standing outside of the royal kingdom with the bloody red cross was me. The bloody cross was a representation of the blood of Jesus Christ, and that I was marked by God in the spirit. The demonic figure that was pacing back and forth was a gatekeeper and he was assigned by Satan to monitor me. Although he was assigned to me he didn't have any legal rights to cross over into my territory or to accuse me of anything until he saw the dagger was lodged in my side.

The dagger that was illuminating in my side gave off a false light that was able to be seen even though it was logged deep inside of me. The dagger also represented Satan's device in my life that he used to penetrate me and gain legal access into my life. Porn was the device that Satan used to open a door to enter into my life. Although I was a watchman myself, I didn't have any authority to confront him because I was partaker of his devices. Not only was I using Satan's devices, but his device became a part of me and I grew numb and eventually unaware that the dagger was even inside of me.

This is why the man in the black suit who was Satan had the ability to enter into my territory and walk right through, unchecked (see 2 Corinthians 2:11).

Children of God it is extremely important to know there's nothing hidden in the spirit. As scripture states, "for everything that is hidden will eventually be brought into the open, and every secret will be brought to the light" (Mark 4:22 NLT).

If and when you're using Satan's device, he knows you're using it. It is also important to know that God assigns angels to our lives to help us in this life (See Hebrews 1:7, 1:14). Satan tries to mimic God by assigning demons, evil spirits, familiar spirits to your life. His sole purpose is to make sure you do not inherit the life God has preordained for you. Sadly, he knows he's incapable of doing that so he has to use you to destroy you.

He does this by getting you to open doors in your life through repeated cycles of sin. Once he gets you in the cycles of sin the next thing he does is what I like to call the sedation process. He puts your senses to sleep by numbing your mind to the point where you can't feel anything anymore. In other words, your inward conviction lessens, it is harder to hear the voice of God, and your awareness of the spiritual realm around you becomes obsolete. All this is done so that you can remain carnal minded. A man that is carnal minded seeks to satisfy the desires of his flesh. Up until that point Satan had done a good job of keeping me mentally incarcerated within my own mind, and as result he gained more territory in other areas of my life.

After he walked through, Satan was able to enter the meeting room unnoticed. I was supposed to be the watchman that guarded the royal gates, but I allowed the enemy to enter because of my association with him. Satan's goal was not just to attack me but to attack everything around me to gain more territory in my life, and those that were connected to me. The demonic figures that were on the horses were principalities that were given deeds to conquer and rule more territory due to the continuous sinning in that particular region. I noticed if there was no enemy within, the enemy outside could do no harm until you allowed him in.

While in the courtroom the Holy spirit began to unveil that the judge was God the father, although I couldn't see Him, only the light emulating from the seat was what I was permitted to see. I could feel his overwhelming presence and authority in the courtroom. I learned that Satan was the accuser dressed in black, and he wanted me to pay the ransom for my sins that were on the scroll. My Lawyer that was dressed in white was Jesus Christ. He stood as my representative and advocate with the father. I was a guilty man without Him, and without the drops of his blood on the scroll I would have been found guilty in the heavenly courtroom. Jesus's blood was the only thing that God recognized and was the only thing that stopped me from getting the sentence I deserved. His blood was the power and key to my freedom. It saved me from eternal damnation. I wept uncontrollably.

After the encounter and receiving the revelation of it to its entirety, my world shifted. I met God in a way that changed me forever and I could not ever forget it. An encounter with God changes everything. It leaves a permanent impression on one's life. For example reading about someone vs actually meeting them brings a different level of confidence and assurance to you. You're no longer living in a fictional imaginary world that is far fetched. I thought I knew Jesus but not to the depth of who He really is. This encounter brought me closer into the fullness of knowing who Christ is. I gained insight and vision. I received sight spiritually. My eyes were opened to a completely different reality.

I knew Jesus as a figurehead, but I didn't know His power. As a child, I always had dreams and visions but nothing to the magnitude of this, and they only got stronger over time. I didn't know that I was blind until God opened my eyes to see into the spirit realm. There is nothing hidden in the spirit. It felt more real than this natural world. I was convinced I was in another place. During this time God stripped me of everything that I thought I knew about Him. He shook up the very foundation that I believed in for the past 15 years. The only reality that I knew of the supernatural was reading the Bible. I didn't know I would have an encounter like this myself.

There were many people in the Bible that had encounters with God. Moses had an encounter at the burning bush. Elijah encountered God on the mountain after killing the prophets of Baal. One of the most prominent encounters was Paul while on the road to Damascus. "As he neared Damascus on his journey, suddenly a light from heaven flashed around him. He fell to the ground and heard a voice say to him, "Saul, Saul, why do you persecute me?" (Acts 9:3-4 NIV).

In a few verses after, God spoke to a man named Ananias to go and find Paul so that he could receive his sight. After Ananias received the instructions from the Lord, "Then Ananias went to the house and entered it placing his hands on Saul he said, 'Brother Saul, the Lord – Jesus who appeared to you on the road as you were coming here – has sent me so that you may see again and be filled with the Holy Spirit.' Immediately something like scales fell from Saul's eyes and he could see again" (Acts 9:17-18 NIV).

It is important to note that Paul was a pharisee and he took pride in having Christians murdered. In fact, after receiving authorization from the other Pharisees, while on the road to Damascus, he was headed to go and slaughter more Christians. Little did Paul know that he was about to have the most impactful encounter of his life. He met the very person he was persecuting, Jesus Christ. Paul was blinded by the glory of God. Although he was blinded in the natural, his spiritual eyes opened. After three days, Paul received his natural sight back with the addition of his spiritual sight. Paul later became one of the most powerful -- if not the most powerful -- apostle in the Bible. Paul was a pharisee and just like the pharisees, he was spiritually blinded to the reality of who Jesus Christ was. After this encounter, his spiritual eyes opened, and it changed the trajectory of his entire life.

This encounter propelled Saul to become Paul and ultimately propelled him into his ministry and purpose as an Apostle. It is the belief that due to this encounter Paul walked in any unusual grace. He was touched by God. Paul was blinded by religion that led to his ignorance. After those scales were removed from his eyes, he was able to see the truth (Jesus Christ). Just like Paul, my eyes were shut until God opened them. Everything changed about me. I didn't feel normal or felt like I could just fit in with any and everybody. Not that I thought that I was better than anyone, but I knew God had chosen me for a special purpose.

INTRUDER

As the fast continued what I thought to be strange occurrences started to happen to me. By the fifth day I wasn't just having dreams at night, but I was having open visions while I was awake. It was like I was seeing with two sets of eyes. I thought I was hallucinating, but the things I saw were so vivid, and clear. It was like watching a 3D movie. Imagine walking in your home at night while it was completely dark, and with the click of the light switch it all changed instantly. It was like night and day.

While I was in my room meditating, I saw a stray dog wandering in front of a family's house. The family felt bad for the dog and put food outside for it. After a few occurrences of this happening the family decided to let the dog into their home. They treated the stray dog like family. They cleaned the dog, fed it, and slept with it. One day the family decided they would get rid of the dog but found it very difficult to do so. The dog had figured out each one of the members of the family, and used it to its advantage to win them over.

By this time I had a pretty consistent routine of writing everything down. I didn't try to figure out what things meant, but I would simply yield to the Holy Spirit to interpret it for me. If you know the story, you may recall Genesis 40:8 Pharaoh's cupbearer and baker were placed in prison under Joseph's watch. He saw that they were distressed, and they said unto him, "We have dreamed a dream, and there is no interpreter of it." And Joseph said unto them, "Do not all interpretations belong to God?."

As I began writing the revelation began to flow out of me as God spoke to me. The dog was a representation of Satan, and how he is a wolf in sheep's clothing. Satan likes to pretend to be something that he's

not in order to gain an advantage over you. I then heard the words "fight for territory". The enemy seeks to gain territory by entering the lives of people. God seeks to advance his kingdom through you and me on the earth, and Satan seeks to advance his kingdom the same way. In this case it was an entire family.

It's elementary for us to think that the devil just wants to attack us, but his goal is to attack your entire bloodline. When the family tried to get rid of the dog it was hard to do so, because it had become a stronghold in their life. The longer you wait to get rid of something that God didn't ordain the stronger the hold becomes. The function of the stronghold is to hold you bound and captive in an area of your life. A person is like a house with many doors. When one lets demonic spirits in, these same spirits seek to take up residence in that home. Like most dogs, they typically pee in certain areas of the house to mark their territory. It's their way of letting you know that this particular part of the house or yard belongs to them.

As the owner of the house you have the ability to remove everything in the house that does not belong there. God has given us the authority according to scripture. "Truly I tell you, whatever you bind on earth will be bound in heaven, and whatever you loose on earth will be loosed in heaven" (Matthew 18:18 NIV). We have the ability through Jesus to serve our addictions, bad habits, thoughts, anxiety, fear, and any stronghold an eviction notice.

There were many other areas of my life that needed fixing. Pornography was only one of them. I still had mother wounds, anxiety, fear of failure, abandonment, and rejection issues. God didn't want me to just have partial deliverance in one area of my life; He wanted me to be completely free. Every word God spoke to me was like arrows piercing my soul. God saw everything in me that man could not see. All these things that I subconsciously buried in the back of my mind for years, God began to expose. For the first time in a long time, I felt naked and fully exposed with nothing to hide. God is all knowing, and his eyes are everywhere. There is truly nothing hidden from Him. He truly knows every part of our being, even those things that we think we are hiding.

It was like being on the operating table and God cutting me with a scalpel. It didn't feel good, in fact it was quite painful, but I knew it was for my good. It was like dying a slow death. My old man had to die and I had to become the man he had predestined me to be. No longer would He allow me to put Band-Aids on open wounds. For example, if I cut down a tree, and don't destroy the roots, the tree will grow back again. If I destroy the root of the tree, it'll be gone forever. Up until this point I mastered cutting down trees, but I didn't know how to deal with the roots.

I looked free, but there were still underlying issues beneath the surface. Not only did this vision show me that I still had strongholds in my life but He showed me where they were coming from. There were certain problems in my life that started at birth. The spirit of rejection and abandonment started early on. The trauma of my mother leaving me started in my adolescent years. The family in the vision represented my family, and that certain strongholds have been lingering around for generations. When we don't deal with the problems in our family they are usually passed down to our children, and they are stuck fighting the devils we should have dealt with. I wasn't just being delivered of my demons, but generational demons that have been in my family for years.

At this point in my fast, I was diving deeper and deeper into the Word of God. I had never felt so energized and enthused to read the Word of God like this before. I didn't eat much throughout my fast but I ate spiritual food instead. I feasted on the scriptures daily, for breakfast, lunch, and dinner. I was determined to get everything out of it. This fast wasn't just about me but I made it about Him; and the byproduct of that was receiving all that I was looking for in Him.

When we seek God first, according to Matthew 6:33, you not only receive God but all the goodness and promises that come with seeking Him. Near the end of my fast, never ever had I felt so free and light in my life. It was like being on cloud 9. It showed me the value of seeking the presence of God more than anything else. I didn't know much about deliverance and neither had I seen it in my church.

I learned that being in the presence of God was and is the secret to wholeness. I didn't know any fancy prayers and I didn't have any deliverance books. All I had was His presence. Deliverance becomes easy when you get in the presence of God. I truly learned how easy deliverance can be when you finally get to Jesus. Like the woman with the issue of blood, when she touched the hem of His garment, she instantly received a miracle. If we let Him, Jesus takes the work out of it. Things become easier when we decide to give it all to Jesus. If we let Him, His spirit will lead us to the path of deliverance.

MORE LIFE

After the fast ended, there was still work that needed to be done. There was one more thing that God wanted from me. It was time for me to break up with my girlfriend. With all the revelatory knowledge that I received on my fast, I was still struggling with this one. I was stuck between a rock and a hard place but I knew I had to do what I had to do. There was no way this cup was going to pass me by. I decided I would do what most young Christians do, "Lord give me one more sign." You know what they say, "be careful what you wish for," because you just might get it. I took a nap later that day and I had a dream my girlfriend was cheating on me. I wanted to brush it off. I thought maybe I was just hallucinating and was just trying to find an excuse to get rid of her, but I knew there was a deeper meaning to it. By this time, God was speaking to me pretty frequently in dreams and visions, so I didn't take it lightly. I knew if God wanted to get His point across, this was the way He would do it. This was one of His primary ways of communicating to me. I didn't confront her directly, but I wanted to confirm that it was true. I logged into her email and scrolled down her mailbox. After scrolling, I saw that she was on a dating app talking to other men. Little did I know, I was funding it. I called her and confronted her about it. She was open and honest and admitted to all of it. I broke it off with her shortly after that conversation. I told my family about it and they were pretty devastated. They actually liked her. I know my dad thought that maybe she could be the one and so did I. The next day Dominique and I were having a conversation about everything that happened and let's just say, he was not a fan of her anymore. My friends and family are harsh on the people that cross me. It's a protective thing. Dominique and I went to my old high school to train that afternoon. It was freezing cold outside and it just snowed the day before, but we were determined to get on the field. We were both outside shoveling snow off the field. Talk about determination. I still wanted to be a professional football player by any means necessary. After a long and intense workout in the freezing cold, I got a call from the general manager of the Toronto Argonauts offering me a contract for the upcoming season. Dominique was more happy for me than I was. He was leaping for joy. You would've thought he was the one they sent the contract to.

On my way home while driving, it dawned on me how quick God can turn things around when you obey Him. I asked myself, "what if I would've listened a long time ago? Where would I be?"

I knew I couldn't change the past but I could only be better for my future. It taught me how to be still and wait on the Lord no matter how difficult the situation may be. When I got home, I was eager to tell my dad that I finally got my contract. His response was, "how much are you going to be making?"

I can't lie, I was pretty salty about that. That was not the response that I was looking for. I thought he would've said something like "I'm proud of you", or "congratulations." I didn't have much to say after that. I didn't want to let it ruin my moment. This was a big accomplishment for me, and I didn't want to let anymore take it away from me. This is something that I wanted to do for me. This was my dream and not theirs. It would've been foolish of me to think that my dad didn't care, just not as much as I did.

Finally, I felt like I could breathe. It felt like a weight was lifted off of my shoulder. No it wasn't the NFL, but I felt like this was a stepping stone to get there. Besides, it wasn't just about football anymore, but ministry. I was a new man with a new purpose to advance the kingdom of God into the arenas of football and the marketplace. God gave me a burning passion to see men saved. A week later, I quit my day job to focus on training full time. My parents weren't too fond of the idea but I felt that it was the right thing to do. I only had about a month before I had to report for training camp in Toronto. Midweek before the training camp, I got a call from Matt saying Toronto had just offered him a contract. I was filled with so much joy after I got the news that I would be playing football with my best friend again. I was convinced God already had this story written out. Not too long after, I was on a flight headed to Toronto for training camp. All I could think was "lights, camera, action baby!"

TORONTO2X

When I arrived in Canada, it was my second time overseas and the immigration line was the back of the building. I thought to myself, "how long is this going to take?" After making a phone call to the team manager, I was at the front of the line in no time and on my way to the team hotel. When I got upstairs to my room, I walked in and in there was Matt. We were roommates again just like old times. We laughed and joked around all night. Both of our lives were sporadic. We didn't know what God had up His sleeve next but whatever it was, we knew it had to be something good. We thought to ourselves, how could we be at the same place at the same time, doing the same exact thing we were doing in college. Playing the sport we love, and winning souls for Jesus. I couldn't have asked for a better life.

The next morning, we all loaded up on the bus and headed over to the team facility. When we got there, we broke off into position meetings. After position meetings, we had team meetings before we hit the practice field. I can't lie, it felt good being around a team atmosphere again. I felt like I was right where I needed to be. When practice ended, we all headed back to the team hotel and decided to go out in the city that night.

Toronto was a sight to see. The city was clean and vibrant. The people were friendly and very welcoming. Matt and I were soaking up every bit of it. We didn't stay out too late because we had to be up early the next morning for practice.

About a week went by and I was getting the hang of things. Cuts were being made every day. Although I was enjoying being around my new teammates, it was hard to get close to them because you didn't know if you would see them the next day. Before we went to our position meeting, I saw Matt clearing out his locker. My heart sank to my stomach. I already knew what time it was. When I got to the practice field, I didn't see him, so I knew he had been released from the team. It was hard for me to focus at practice knowing my best friend was just released. While on the bus back to the hotel, I was staring at my window, looking like a sad puppy.

When I got upstairs to my room, Matt left sticky notes on my bed leaving me behind with some encouraging words. I thought it was very selfless of him to think about me after getting released from the team. It's hard to come across genuine people like Matt, but when you do, you want them in your corner. Training camp was coming to an end and our first preseason game was around the corner. I was excited and couldn't wait to get back in front of the crowd again.

Finally, it was here. The day of my first professional football game. We had morning meetings to put finishing touches on our gameplan. My coaches told me that I would receive a lot of playing time in the game. I took it with a grain of salt. I didn't want to get my hopes too high to be let down. Before you know it, it was almost kick off time. My heart was beating through my chest. I hadn't been this nervous in a long time. The first quarter went by before my number was called. My coach came over and tapped me on the helmet, "you're up son."

After I got in the game, I caught my first pass for a first down. Shortly after, all the nerves went away and the rest was history. I had one more preseason game to make one final impression on the team before final cuts. I attacked that week of practice aggressively. I wasn't going to let anything stand in the way of me making the team. While in my position meeting, the day before the game, I felt really uneasy. For some strange reason, I felt my time on the team was coming to an end. I was perplexed because I just had a good game the week before.

In my anger I asked God, "why did you bring me here?"

In a gentle whisper, I heard Him say, "to learn."

I thought to myself, "what more was there to learn that I didn't already know?"

I brushed it off and told myself, "I'll have the best game of my life tomorrow and there's no way they can get rid of me."

Gameday was here and it was time to shine. I got on the team flight dressed to impress. You know the motto, "when you look good you feel good, when you feel good you play good, and when you play good they pay good." After a long flight, we landed in Calgary.

When I got off the plane I thought to myself, "I haven't felt this good in a long time."

I was feeling like my old self again. First play of the game, I scored my first touchdown but it was called back. When we got back into the huddle, my coach called the same play. I scored another touchdown. My teammates and I were hyped. After that series ended, we were back on the field and my coach called my number again. I scored another touchdown. I had the game of my life. I called my dad after the game and told him how well it went. He was excited for me. I thought to myself, "it's only up from here."

I woke up early the next morning to get breakfast and saw several of my teammates packing their bags. I knew there was no way I was going to get called into the office after the game that I just had. I knew my spot was secured. Little did I know, I was next to be released from the team.

About 20 minutes later, I got a call from a Canadian number. It was the general manager calling me into his office. He told me to bring my playbook with me. If you know anything about football, before you get cut, they always ask for the playbook back, so I already knew my fate. After a short conversation with the Gm and my head coach, they released me from the team. I walked out of the meeting room frustrated, angry, and with my face held down. It was like Deja vu all over again. One heartbreak after another. I think one of the worst things a person can go through is get so close to their dream and watch it shatter before their eyes. I had been building this dream for a very long time and here I was watching it crumble, again.

When I got upstairs, I was still in a state of shock. They gave me 45 minutes to pack my bags and be downstairs to ride the taxi back to the airport so I didn't have much time to think about what just happened. I called my dad to let him know that I was being released from the team. It was quiet on the phone. It was like taking the air out of the stadium at an away game on a game winning drive.

Suddenly, his next words were, "okay, it's time to get a job."

FAMILY FEUD

When I got back home, tensions were high with my parents. I decided to stay with my Uncle Corey, my dad's youngest brother, for a few days until things calmed down. I was pretty upset at my dad for the way he responded to me while we were on the phone in Toronto after I was released from the team. I worked so hard to finally get that opportunity to play on the professional level, and I felt like he just disregarded my feelings and all that I was going through in that moment. This wasn't the first occurrence. I was already on edge, but this was my tipping point.

I felt like getting a job would always be there, but we only get one opportunity to live out our dreams. It wasn't a matter of whether my dad loved me or not, I knew he loved me, but I came to the realization that my dream was mine and not his. If you know me, then you know that I am not a person that likes conflict, especially with the people that I love. I knew going home would only make matters worse. My parents were adamant about me quitting football and pursuing a different career and I strongly disagreed.

This was probably one of the lowest moments of my life. I needed somewhere where I could lay low for a couple of days and get my thoughts together. Things were happening so fast and it was hard for me to comprehend it all. I wanted to collect myself and I felt like the best place to do that was at my uncle's house.

I needed to be loved and not pressured into making my next decision. I also needed time to heal. It was like I was walking through a maze blindfolded and I didn't know which step to take next. Everywhere I turned, I was being diverted in a different direction. One minute I was here and the next minute I was there.

I tried consulting God but He was silent. I knew it was only a matter of time before He gave me some direction. I think one of the hardest things a person can go through is learning how to handle the silence of God in a tough situation.

After a couple of days of being at my uncle's house, I fell into a deep depression. I didn't eat much, and I came out of my room here and there. I slept for about 14 hours a day, hoping to sleep the pain away. I logged off all my social media accounts because I didn't want anyone to question why I was back home. The worst part of it all was feeling like a failure. In my head, I let my family, friends, and ultimately myself down.

My back was against the wall and it was as if God was nowhere to be found. I kept knocking, but my knocks weren't being answered. After about the 5th day of lying in bed all day, God finally spoke. He said, "go lower."

Let's just say, that's not what I wanted to hear. I thought to myself, "how much lower can I go?"

I mean in my eyes this was rock bottom. I wanted to cry all over again, but I knew it wasn't going to solve anything. God didn't want my tears, He wanted my obedience. I couldn't stop pondering on the thoughts of the last words He spoke to me while I was in Toronto. I remember asking Him why He brought me there and He responded, "to learn." I thought to myself, "what exactly did He want me to learn?"

Later that day, I decided to go back home and have a conversation with my parents about what I was going through. When I got to the house, I tried to put my code in to get inside but it wasn't working. I called my dad to see why my code wasn't working. After about 5 or 6 calls, I received a long text message stating that they were at Texas State dropping off my little sister and that they changed the code to the house. They also stated that I was not allowed in the house until they returned. At this point, I was done with my family. Luckily I had a few bags of clothes already packed in my car from Toronto. I don't get angry often but at this point, I was at a 10.

When I got back to my uncle's house, we talked for a couple of hours. He agreed that I could stay for as long as I needed. I was in hopes that a team would call me soon so I didn't have any intentions on staying long. I figured maybe a few weeks at the most. A few weeks went by and still no calls. At this point, I just about gave up completely on ever playing again. I was running low on cash and in dire need of a job. I filled out a few applications online and within a day, Dominique and I had an interview at a clothing distribution center.

We both got the job and started working a few days after. The job wasn't hard at all. We drove around the building and sorted clothes into carts. It's funny how things can turn around quickly. We talked every day about how we both felt like we didn't belong there. Dominique and I made the best of our situation, but we knew we wouldn't be there long.

My uncle Corey was working at a tailoring company and wanted me to come work with him. It didn't take me long to jump ship. I've always been good with my hands and I had desires of starting a clothing brand one day. This was the perfect gig to get some experience. While working the tailoring job I learned a lot of skills. The job was a lot more laid back. It was the right environment for me. It wasn't the ideal job that I wanted, but I made the most of it. I walked in every day with a smile on my face, but deep down I was still hurting and depressed.

A RUN IN WITH FEAR

One day after work, I went home to take a nap, I fell into a deep sleep and I began to dream again. In my dream, I was walking through the city of New York minding my business. While walking, I arrived at this humongous skyscraper building. I noticed there was a ladder in front of the building and if I wanted to, I could climb to the top of it. I thought to myself, "why not?" so I began climbing. Eventually, I climbed all the way to the top of the building.

I stepped out onto the rooftop and glanced around the building. I could see all of Manhattan from here. It was a beautiful sight. I decided to walk to the edge of the roof, sat and let my feet dangle off the building. I sat there for a moment and thought to myself, "is this it? I climbed all the way to the top for this?"

It was the emptiest feeling ever. Within a split second, I remembered that I was afraid of heights. All of a sudden I started to panic. I stood up and walked away from the edge of the building. When I turned around, I was met by a gruesome demonic spirit. I can't put into words how horrendous he looked but I was startled by it. It began to speak to me and remind me of all of my failures, my fear of heights, and all the negative thoughts that I once had. When the demon spoke, his words paralyzed me. I was on the ground in a fetal position, shaking in fear. I knew it was only a matter of time before he killed me. The more he spoke, the worse it got. In the middle of him talking, I noticed he never physically touched me. He was just speaking words that were causing me to be in a paralyzed state.

Eventually, I gained the strength to stand up and confront it and he went away. I walked over to the side of the building where the ladder was to head back down the building. When I got there I noticed that the ladder was cut in half. I woke up. When I woke up, I grabbed my dream book. I started to pray and ask God for the interpretation of the dream. As I wrote the dream out, the revelation came. The Holy Spirit spoke to me letting me know what all of the symbols in the dream meant. In the dream, I finally reached a place where I've always wanted to be. The ladder was a representation of the upward path that I would take to get there. After taking that path, I finally made it to the top. For a moment, while I was at the top, I was happy, excited and full of joy. Then suddenly familiar thoughts started to plague my mind. Everything that I could possibly be afraid of entered into my mind. When I turned around, I saw the spirit of FEAR waiting to torment me.

For one, I didn't know that fear was a spirit and secondly, I noticed that he met me at the top. Reaching the top was a representation of achieving all my goals and accomplishments. What I didn't know was that the driving force behind my ambition to make it was fear. The fear of failure, fear of man, and fear of not living up to my full potential. I had given my life over to fear. Instead of love (love of God) being the driving force, it was fear. I noticed that fear was only as effective as I allowed it to be. When I came to the realization that fear had no power, I was able to stand to my feet and confront it.

The Bible tells us, "if we resist the devil, he will flee" (James 4:7 NIV). When I got to the side of the building where the ladder was, I tried to go back down the path that I came up. Only this time, the spirit of fear took a chunk of the ladder with it. The ladder was built on fear and my way up was faulty, shaky, never firm from the beginning, so he took what was his.

This revelation showed me that everything should be done out of love and not fear (see 2 Timothy 1:7). We must ask ourselves what's really the driving force(s) behind our decision making. We cannot build on a faulty foundation. Building without God is building to fail. Although we may have dreams, goals and aspirations, to reach the top we have to make sure that our motives are pure in the process. After receiving this revelation and pondering on it, I realized that maybe it was good that things happened the way they did. Although I would've had what I ultimately wanted, I still would've been empty inside.

This changed my perspective on everything since Toronto. I slowly felt a weight being lifted off my shoulders. The dark cloud that was over me was finally starting to leave. Later that night I called Matt and told him about the dream. We talked all night about it. It gave him a different perspective on life and what he was going through as well. Besides, we were pretty much walking in the same shoes.

While we were on the phone, Matt suggested that I move to Houston. This wasn't the first time he mentioned it to me since I came back from Toronto. I thought maybe this was God speaking through Matt to get to me. Although it sounded good, I was comfortable in Dallas-Fort Worth. I didn't want to leave home. For some strange reason, after we got off the phone, I thought maybe he was right, and Houston could be my next destination.

Early the next morning, my uncle came into my room to wake me up for work. God knows I was never a morning person.

"You want some breakfast?" He yelled from across the room.

"Yes, sir I do," I replied. I

could never resist my uncle's food. He's always been one of our family's best cooks, and he could make a mean breakfast. Most people in Louisiana are born with a spatula in their hand. It doesn't take long before we're in the kitchen cooking family recipes. When we sat down at the table he asked if I had heard from my dad.

"No I haven't," I responded.

"You should give him a call," he stated.

"I'll think about it unc," I replied.

Calling my dad was the last thing on my mind. I brushed it off and started eating.

"You put your foot in these jalapeno cheese grits!"

"I know, tell me about it, nephew," uncle responded.

My uncle and I always had a tight relationship since I was younger. He's always been my favorite uncle on my dad's side.

Little did my uncle know that I had a surprise waiting for him at work. I went out and bought him some gifts for his birthday. I got all the co-workers together to throw a surprise party for his birthday at work. When we got there, everybody was all dressed up and waiting for us to enter the building. As we entered where everybody was, they all yelled "Surprise!" My uncle was smiling ear to ear. It was such a joy to see him happy. I handed him his gift and after opening it, he started crying. "Thanks nephew, you don't know how much this means to me," he said. "It's all love unc," I replied.

After we finished celebrating my uncle's birthday, we headed back to our stations to finish the rest of the day at work. For some reason I couldn't get that conversation Matt and I had out of my head. My days at work were always sporadic because I was a floater. I pretty much helped wherever they needed me, whether it was unloading boxes, sorting clothes, sewing, or taking measurements from time to time.

My coworkers were all nice and loved having fun. It made every day go by much quicker. I really enjoyed working with my uncle because he would buy me lunch every day. It wasn't my dream job, but I enjoyed every minute of it. Plus, I was learning a lot of skills about sewing from my uncle.

Dominique called me later that day and told me he quit that job. I knew it was only a matter of time before he did. He said he was going to pursue personal training full time. I've always told him he should pursue training. I have always been an advocate for chasing your dreams. I don't think anyone should live with regret knowing that they didn't pursue what they love the most.

One of my favorite speakers Les Brown once said that "the richest place on the planet is the graveyard." There are so many people that have died not living up to their full potential. I believe that one of the worst human experiences a person can have is dying with their gifts inside of them and never releasing it to the world. When God imparts gifts into us, it's His gift to us but what we do with it should be our gift back to Him (see Matthew 13).

THE RAFT

A couple of days passed, and thoughts of playing football again began creeping into my mind. I trained regularly, just in case I received a phone call to come back and play. After a long day at work, I returned home, took a long, hot shower, and then read my Bible. While studying the book of Matthew, I suddenly slipped into a vision.

In this vision, I found myself in a raft, floating in the middle of the ocean. Clutched in my hand was a handheld pole with a net attached to its top. As I drifted, I spotted a beautiful fish in the water, and I eagerly lowered my hand in hopes of capturing it. To my surprise, the fish slipped through the net. In disbelief, I tried again and again, but each attempt left me empty-handed. Eventually, I decided to inspect the net and discovered a hole in it. I wondered how this could have happened when, in an instant, a massive boat appeared on the horizon, approaching me. As I gazed at the boat, I noticed a man with an appearance of pure radiance standing on it. In the blink of an eye, I found myself aboard the ship, as if I was transported.

The man was dressed in a beautiful white garment with a sash around his waist. His hair flowed to his shoulders, and his face glowed with light. I marveled at the sight, astonished that I could be in the presence of such brilliance and still be alive. I likened it to staring at the sun from ten feet away without being obliterated. I couldn't believe it, but I was standing before Jesus. I couldn't discern his facial features; his face was veiled by the intense light. Moments later, he glanced at me and lowered a massive net into the waters. As he did so, the boat leaned to the left where the net was deployed. When he raised the net back up, it was overflowing with fish.

In this vision, Jesus spoke to me, explaining that the fish I had seen in the water symbolized football—the one fish I cared about the most. He allowed me to pursue it, knowing that I would not catch it, to teach me a lesson. I had become so consumed with trying to catch that one fish that I failed to recognize the abundance of other fish in the sea around me. Stubbornly, I persisted in chasing after football without investigating why it eluded me. It wasn't until I discovered the hole in the net that I ceased my pursuit.

Jesus had deliberately placed the hole to show me that there were more fish to catch than just football. I had been blinded by my pride and selfish ambition, unwilling to explore the vast seas of other gifts, talents, skills, and abilities hidden within me. Jesus had to reveal this truth to me, as our lives are hidden in Him. When I encountered Jesus, I realized that I didn't have to overexert myself to achieve everything. I had wasted so much time and energy trying to do things my way instead of being obedient to His plan. We often forge our paths, neglecting to seek God for the path He has predestined for us. Psalm 37:23-24 proclaims that the steps of a good man are ordered by the Lord. Only when I grasped this concept could I cease coming up empty-handed.

Upon exiting the vision, Jesus led me to read Luke 5:4-11, and it resonated deeply within me. The scripture recounted a story of Simon Peter, who, at Jesus' command, put out into deep water and let down the nets for a catch. Although they had toiled all night with no success, when they obeyed Jesus, they caught an overwhelming number of fish. It was a moment of realization for Simon Peter, who fell to his knees, acknowledging his sinfulness in the presence of such divine power. In response, Jesus reassured him, saying, "Don't be afraid; from now on you will fish for people." Upon hearing these words, Simon Peter and his companions left everything behind to follow Jesus.

This scripture now became more tangible and real to me than life itself, especially after the profound encounter I had just experienced. It was time for me to lay down my life and follow Him. God had a grander purpose for my life; it was time to relinquish my struggle for football and allow Him to make me a fisher of men.

GREYHOUND

Matt called me shortly after and we spoke about the move to Houston. I was still feeling uneasy about it. I didn't like being out of my comfort zone. I was comfortable right where I was in Dallas-Ft. Worth.

The next day, while getting ready for work I went outside to warm my car up, and it wouldn't start. I just had work done on it a few days ago. I towed it over to a shop to let someone look at it. While speaking with the mechanic he told me that the car was pretty much done for. My heart sunk in my stomach. Here we go again. Shortly after I called my Uncle to have him come pick me up for work. I was moping around all day at work. Work was slow so I decided I would take an early lunch. My uncle had ordered him and me some wings.

I was munching away when I heard God say, "you have two days to move to Houston".

I thought to myself, “how can I move to Houston without a car?”

I tried to ignore what God said but then out of nowhere Matt sent me a text letting me know that his dad called him asking if I had packed my bags for Houston yet. When I got home that night, I tried to sleep but I couldn’t. I kept feeling God nudging on me. He wouldn’t let me get comfortable.

Finally, I told myself, “well maybe it’s time for me to leave.”

I woke up and packed my bags within an hour. I went to my uncle’s room to let him know I was moving. I knew he would be caught off guard because I never mentioned Houston to him. I told him that it was something that I had to do and by the look on his face, I could tell he was sad that I was leaving. I called my boss to let her know that I was leaving. She told me to give her a call if I needed anything. I didn’t have much money to get a car, so my only way to Houston was on a bus. Shortly after, Dominique came to pick me up because he was taking me to the bus station the next morning. While I was at Dominique’s house, we made dinner and watched Sportscenter until it was time for bed. I was pretty spaced out about all that was going on. I felt like everything was being rushed and I didn’t have enough time to prepare for it. I asked God why it was so urgent for me to move but I didn’t get a response.

Dominique and I got up early the next morning to head to the bus station.

We stopped and got some breakfast on the way. I didn’t really have much of an appetite, so I didn’t eat much. I can’t lie, I was pretty nervous about the move. I knew my whole life was about to change. Dominique dropped me off at the bus station and gave me some words of encouragement before I left. God knew I needed it. It had been years since

I was on a bus and I wasn't looking forward to the long ride. Shortly after, I was on my way to Houston with only $11 to my name.

HOUSTON

I finally arrived in Houston and Matt was waiting for me at the bus station. Outside of Dominique, Matt knew me better than anybody. Boy was I excited to see him. It had been a while since we last saw each other. I considered Matt like a brother to me. He was more than just a friend. Blood couldn't make us any closer. We definitely had a David and Jonathan relationship.

I believe there are certain areas in your life that don't flourish until you meet the people that God has assigned to your life to help you.

Our lives were intertwined in such a way that couldn't be put into words. Ever since the day we first met at TJC, we hadn't missed a beat. He's always been there for me in my toughest moments and I was always there for him.

"What's wrong?" he asked.

By then I was spaced out throughout our conversation staring at the window. "Oh. nothing," I replied.

"You sure? Look man everything is going to be okay. I know this is new for you, but God has everything under control. You got a place to stay, food to eat, and an opportunity to get on your feet," he said. "Just trust it. I know it'll take some time getting used to," he continued.

"Anyways, you want something to eat?" he asked.

"Yea let's go to the Rally's," I responded.

After grabbing a bite to eat, we headed back to his parent's house. When I walked in, I was greeted with lots of love from his mom and dad.

I've always loved Mr. Davis. He's always treated me like family. He's one of the most genuine men that I know.

"You need help carrying your bags upstairs? The guest room is upstairs. It's all ready to go," he said.

I was tired from the long bus ride, so I went upstairs to shower before bed. While in the shower, I felt a strong urge to call my dad. I felt the same thing on the bus ride there. I knew it was the Holy Spirit speaking to me. I went to bed that night with so much on my mind wondering how everything was going to pan out in Houston. I mean I didn't have much, the only thing I was clinging on to was the Word of God. This was one of the biggest moments of my life concerning my faith.

All I knew to do was keep walking in the direction that He laid out before me. Even though I felt like at times He let me down, there was still a driving force in me telling me to keep following His direction. I slept in that morning but when I woke up, I gave my dad a call. It was the first time we had spoken in about two months. I called him to let him know that I had officially moved to Houston. I could hear in his voice that he was sad about it.

One thing my dad always took pride in was looking out for his kids. My dad didn't have the easiest childhood growing up. My grandpa wasn't in his life for the majority of it so he took pride in making sure that he was always present. We weren't on the phone long but we were on long enough to sort out our differences.

He made it clear that I could always come home if I needed to. I thought about it but I knew Houston was the place that I needed to be. I still had more self-discovery that I needed to do. Later, Matt and I drove around Houston with Mr. Davis.

While in the car, Mr. Davis said to me "I know this is all new for you, but everything is going to be okay. You're in good hands. You don't have to pay for anything while you're here. I just want to help you get to where you need to be.

"Don't feel like you're a burden on anybody. We are blessed to have you," he said.

Hearing those words definitely took a weight off of my shoulders. I felt like I could finally breathe.

"What's your credit score?" He asked.

"I don't know, Mr. Davis. I honestly don't know," I said.

"Okay when we get back to the house, we'll take a look at it and see where you're at," he responded.

We went the rest of the day playing games, laughing, and carrying on. I wasn't much of a dominoes player so I would sit and watch Matt and his dad play. They always were very competitive at everything they did. Shortly after, Mr. Davis called me upstairs to finish the conversation we had earlier in the car.

"Okay son, just wanted to let you know that I love you and I'm happy you're here. I'm here to help you. Let's look at your credit and let's put a plan in action to get you going on the right track," he said.

We sat down and wrote out a plan so I could get a job, purchase a car, and my first home. After our meeting ended, I went to bed because we had church early in the morning. I remember Matt raving about his church so I couldn't wait to experience it. We got up early that next morning and got some hot and fresh Shipley donuts. Man, they were finger lickin'! God knows I love me some Shipley's. Best donuts in the world if you ask me. If you get there early in the morning, you can get a fresh batch right out of the oven.

When we got to church, praise & worship had already started. We walked in and made our way to the front and sat in the second row on the far left side of the sanctuary. When I sat down, I could feel God's presence around me. I knew I was exactly where I needed to be. After the praise team sung, the Pastor preached a phenomenal message. Shortly after, he asked for a seed offering of $11. When I reached in my pocket, I pulled out a $10 bill and a $1 bill. At that moment it dawned on me that this was the exact amount of money that I had to my name.

I knew it had to be God. I didn't hesitate to give it. I leaned over and whispered to Matt, "bro, I have $11 to my name."

We both agreed that it had to be God. When we left church we stopped at Timmy Chan's to get something to eat. I always loved some fried chicken wings and shrimp fried rice. It has always been one of my favorite things to eat. When we got home, we ate and talked about the service at church. I knew God was about to turn things around in my life but I still had my reservations.

The following day I woke up early and started hammering away at job applications. Sometime during, Matt came in the room and told me that a friend of his was on the way and he was raving that I met him. Not too long after, he came to the house, came upstairs and introduced himself.

"Hey, I'm Donovan. Nice to meet you," he said.

Let's just say one conversation led to another and before you know it, we connected. Somewhere in the conversation, Matt brought up work and the possibility of Donovan helping me get a gig with Enterprise rent-a-car. When we were finished conversing, we went to grab a bite to eat.

I hit the sheets (went to sleep) shortly after we got back. Two days passed and I got a call from Ross. I went in for an interview later that day and started working the following day. I figured this would be my best bet until I got another gig. Besides, I knew I wasn't going to be there long. I just wanted to put some cash in my pocket for the time being. Ross was the best option because it was in walking distance in the back of the neighborhood. It had been a while since I was without a car. I felt like I was back to humble beginnings. I walked every day, and while walking I contemplated on the Goodness of God.

It made me appreciate simple things a lot more. It reinforced to me that things could be taken away in a heartbeat. You have things one day and the next day you don't (see James 4:14). Two weeks went by working at Ross and let's just say, I was fed up with it. I got my first check and it was just enough to make ends meet.

One day while walking home from work, when I got in the driveway, I got a call from Enterprise letting me know that they wanted to offer me a job. It was a breath of fresh air and a sigh of relief. Finally, I could get some real money coming in. I knew I wouldn't be a millionaire, but I would be making more money than I'd ever made before. After my onboarding process, I started my first day at Enterprise. It was a really good first day at work.

I enjoyed meeting my new coworkers. Although I'm

an introvert at times, I love meeting new people. Besides, my boss at Enterprise was really dope and I learned a lot from him. I still didn't have a car so Matt would drop me at work every morning. Lord knows I hated being a burden, but he was willing to help me out for the time being. My boss Will would take me home after work if Matt couldn't pick me up.

It seemed like even when I didn't have much, God was still providing. About a month and a half of working at Enterprise, I was able to purchase a car. The next thing on my to-do list was getting my own place. I knew it was only a matter of time before I accomplished it.

GRACE

I went to church regularly, attending service on Sundays and Bible study on Tuesdays. However, due to my demanding work schedule, making it to Tuesday's Bible study became a struggle at times. One Tuesday, Matt called to inquire if I would be attending Bible study that evening. I honestly didn't feel like going, and surprisingly, I didn't feel guilty about it either. Later that day, I ended up not taking a lunch break due to our busy workload, and my boss allowed me to leave an hour early. I decided to head home to take a nap.

But as I drove home, a strong impression grew within me, urging me to go to church instead. I tried to dismiss it, but it intensified the closer I got to my house. Eventually, I made a sharp turn and headed back in the direction of the church. When I arrived, the parking lot was still empty, so I parked at the back of the church to rest briefly. While I closed my eyes, in an attempt to take a quick nap, I was pulled into a vision.

It felt like I was traveling through a whirlwind tunnel, unable to see anything. Then, out of nowhere, I saw Jesus suspended in mid-air with a crown of thorns on His head, and blood streaming down His face. Words could not capture the emotions welling up inside me as I gazed upon Him. The more I looked, the clearer the image became, as if I were adjusting the lenses of a camera. I witnessed an overwhelming amount of pain, agony, and anguish etched upon His face. He gazed at me with a love and passion deeper than anything I had ever experienced before. It was as if a blazing fire raged within His eyes. I stood there, paralyzed like a deer caught in headlights. Without uttering a single word, He conveyed so much to me.

The way He looked at me, with such profound love, was unlike anything I had ever encountered. Simultaneously, He drew me closer to Him. I could sense there was something He wanted me to see. As I continued to study His face, my attention was drawn to the blood dripping down His face. There was something mesmerizing about the blood. I observed words embedded within the droplets of His blood, and I saw the word "Grace." It was as if the word "Grace" was tattooed inside His blood. Suddenly, He pulled me into Himself, and I felt like I was being sucked into a vacuum. In that instant, I began to witness the molecular structure of His DNA. I saw the word "Grace" intricately woven down the strands of His DNA. His blood cells were encoded with Grace—His blood carried the essence of Grace within it.

As I beheld this revelation, I was immediately pulled out of the vision and found myself back in my car. I began to weep uncontrollably as the reality struck me that He shed His precious blood for me. It was a moment likened unto Timothy's encounter in John 20:27 when Jesus allowed him to touch His pierced side after the resurrection. Jesus had allowed me to look within Him. In that beautiful moment, I realized that Grace is not just unmerited favor; Grace is a person, Christ Jesus.

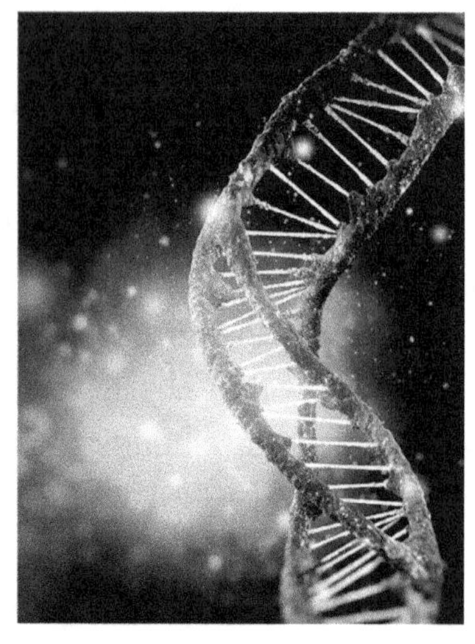

The link between Jesus and Grace is inseparable. When Jesus's blood poured out, so did Grace, because they are inextricably linked. This is why Jesus had to shed His blood for us, no other being in the entire universe could pay such a price. Jesus Himself was the only way! His blood served as the code that decoded the corruption of sin. Encrypted within the blood of Jesus was the answer to all of humanity's predicament. Ephesians 2:8-9 beautifully affirms, "for it is by grace you have been saved, through faith—and this is not from yourselves, it is the gift of God—not by works, so that no one can boast" (NIV). This verse encapsulates the essence of our salvation, highlighting the unmerited favor bestowed upon us by the divine gift of grace, Jesus Christ.

HOME SWEET HOME

The day finally came for me to move into my own place. This was a huge milestone for me. I was so excited. Matt, Donovan, and I loaded my things up into the U-Haul. I purchased some furniture from a nearby store and all I had to do was pick it up and load it into my new place. Another friend's mother had given me some furniture as well. After about 5 hours of moving, we were finished, and I was finally settled into my new place.

A few days later, I met up with Matt and Donovan. We came up with the idea of starting a podcast. We named it *SaltPodcast*. Every time we linked up, we always had interesting conversations whether it was about sports, faith, culture, or just our daily lives. We wanted to create a platform to bring Christ into the culture through conversations. We all pitched in, got our LLC, equipment, and created our social media platform. Not too long after, we released our first episode and it was a major success.

Life in Houston continued as usual. Work, workout, and church. I met some new friends over the past few months and we would all meet up once a week to hang out. This was always the highlight of my week since I was working long hours at Enterprise. I felt like I didn't have a life outside of work. I was also still getting used to living on my own.

I definitely missed being at Matt's parent's house. Whenever I got home from work, Mr. Davis had a hot meal waiting for me. I mean he could cook a mean meatloaf. I told him he would have to give me the recipe one day. He would always laugh and brush me off.

On the flip side, I had my place all to myself. One thing I said I always needed or raved about was peace of mind. Having my own place, I felt like I would finally have it. Besides, I enjoyed being by myself, being introverted at heart. It was also good, because I had time for self-discovery. I was still finding myself without football. I was using this time to learn about the other gifts and talents that God placed in me. It was just me and God. I would often ask Him questions like "why am I here?" "what's my purpose?" In my time alone, I discovered that my purpose was hidden in God and that He had the blueprint to my life. He knew where I'm supposed to go, where I'm supposed to be and ultimately who I'm supposed to become. So it wasn't just self-discovery but it was finding out who I was in Christ Jesus.

During this time, God put it on my heart to reach out to my mother. Let's just say, that was the last thing that I wanted to do. I didn't want any parts of it. I wrestled with God like Jacob did with the angel in Genesis

32. I tried to ignore it as much as I could. I would be at work and it would come up. I would be at church and it would come up. Even when I tried to pray, God would bring it up, and immediately I would shut down and quit praying. It was like he didn't want to talk until I resolved the matter with my mom!

I finally quit fighting and reached out to my mom. I knew having a conversation over the phone wasn't going to suffice. So I decided I would drive down to New Orleans instead. I reached out and told her I would come down that weekend. I still had one foot in and one foot out. I tried to find every excuse not to go. When the day came, I laid in my bed pondering what I would say, and what the conversation would be like between us. I hit the road not too long after, and while still pondering I could hear God saying, "just trust me."

ROAD TO RECOVERY

"Welcome to Louisiana." I saw the sign approaching as I crossed over the state line. You always knew you were in Louisiana by the smell of the swamp waters. It always gave off such a strong odor. I didn't notice it growing up, I guess I was just used to it. I saw nothing but water for miles away. It brought back old memories of hurricane Katrina and just how flooded this highway was.

I was nervous to meet my mom, but I was excited to see my friends and family. I mean it had been over 5 years since I had been back home. Sadly I didn't stay in touch with most of my friends while I was in Texas. I would frequently get calls about some of them going to jail mostly on drug charges, and some of them had been killed. It was never easy getting those phone calls. New Orleans had become the murder capital after hurricane Katrina.

New Orleans had and always will be home, but the thought of moving back was never an option for me. I was just a few miles out from there and I could still see the effects the hurricane had on the city. The Government still hadn't fully restored the city, and the only area that was remodeled was Downtown New Orleans where all the tourist attractions are.

I thought to myself there's still no place like home. I drove through the city, and I could see it was lit up. The smell of the Cajun food, music, and street performers was a site to see. New Orleans has always had some of the most talented and creative musicians. I grew up listening to New Orleans Jazz Music, and the saxophone had always been my favorite instrument. The culture is rich and the food is second to none. I drove by one of my favorite spots before heading to go meet with my mom.

The New Orleans Art district was full of paintings and monuments of our history. If you know anything about me you know that I love art. I sat in the car for about an hour looking at the paintings, and pondering on what I would say to my mom. I thought to myself, "well, here goes nothing," as I drove off, headed to my mom's house.

My mom moved into my grandmother's house after she passed. This was the same house I grew up in. There were so many memories made there on 3rd Emmanuel Street. I finally got to my neighborhood and as I drove in, it was dark at this point. There weren't many streetlights so you couldn't see much. I could still see the effects of the storm on my neighborhood. It didn't look anything like it used to. It almost looked like a ghost town. It was gloomy and I could feel the emptiness and the vacancy as I drove through. It wasn't alive and vibrant like it once was mirroring downtown. As I arrived on 3rd Emmanuel Street, I had several flashbacks of my brother and me running up and down the street when we were younger.

This triggered a well of emotions inside of me. It was at that moment that I knew the little boy in me needed to be healed and set free. I truly felt like I was robbed of my childhood and the time spent with my friends and brother. Knowing some of them I would never see again, because they didn't make it to the age of 21 gave me chills. I felt sadness, guilt, anger and frustration all at once. Some of the worst pain is when you're screaming on the inside, but no one hears you. You're waving for help, but no one sees you. You're praying and hoping that someone or something will save you from the pain you've been sinking in for years.

The little wounded boy in me had been crying for years hoping to be rescued and set free. I was troubled in my soul and it was finally time for restoration. I finally got out of the car and I walked over to the tree where my grandmother and I would sit during the day and night as the train went by. I tried to keep it together but I busted out in tears. No one knew the pain I felt at that moment.

I quickly dried my eyes as I knocked on the door of the house. The last thing I wanted to do was let my mom see me crying. My mom opened the door and I walked into the living room. It was pretty dark in the house but I noticed that she made some renovations to the house. I was pretty upset about it. It didn't look like the last memory that I had of being there.

I sat on the couch and I started watching TV with my mom. She asked me how my trip was and a few other generic questions. I can't lie, it was awkward. Not just for me but for both of us. It was like we were waiting on each other to open up. My uncle Bruce (my mom's youngest brother) walked in on us as we were sitting in the living room. I was excited to see him. My mood went from low to high.

"Hey what's up nephew?" he said.

"Nothing much unc, just happy to be back in the city," I replied. "Oh yea?" he said with his Cajun accent.

I knew my uncle was happy that my mother and I were talking. He always pushed for her and me to have a relationship more than anybody else did.

"Y'all tryna go out tonight?" he asked.

My uncle had always been the life of any party. He never stood in one place long. He's always lived life on the go.

"No unc, not tonight, I'm pretty tired from the drive in. I think I'mma hit the sheets early tonight," I responded.

Truth is I was just emotionally drained and needed to get some rest. I waved goodbye to my uncle and mother and drove up the street to my aunty Adreinan's house.

"Hey my babyyyyyyyyyy! I'm so happy to see you!" she greeted me. She also had a Cajun accent. "Your room in the back. It's cleaned and ready for you. Your bath towel is on the bed and if you need anything let me know," she said.

"Thank you aunty," I responded. "What's that you cookin?" I asked.

"I stayed up cooking some beans. I made a pot of red beans and rice," she responded. "Make sure you get you some after you shower."

After I got out of the shower, I was stuffing my face with food. Everyone knew my aunty could throw down in the kitchen. Saying no to my aunt's cooking is like saying no to Jesus. After I finished eating, I went to my room to go to sleep. I woke up the next morning, brushed my teeth, took a shower, and ate breakfast. My aunty had a hot breakfast waiting on me early that morning. I had plans to go by my mother's house but my aunty asked if I could help set up for the neighborhood reunion. Every year, there was always a neighborhood reunion where everyone from the town came back and partied. I loaded up a few things into the truck and drove to the store to get a couple items for my aunty. When I got back, almost everybody was outside already partying. There were tents set up, food everywhere, trampolines, bounce houses for the kids, music, and the second line band was in full swing. I went inside to change outfits and drove to my mother's house.

When I walked in, I noticed she was still sitting in the dark just watching TV. I asked her if she was going to attend the neighborhood party. Everybody was already asking me about her. I told them I would try my best to get her out of the house. Word on the street was that my mom would just sit in the house all day and not come out.

"No, I think Imma just stay inside," she responded. She asked me, "have you heard from your brother?"

"No, I haven't. He called me, I just never got around to calling him back," I responded.

"Make sure you reach out to him, he's always asking about you," she said.

We sat and watched TV for another 20 minutes.

"Ma, how you feelin?" I asked.

"I'm doing okay," she said.

"You sure?" I asked.

We started conversing and then suddenly she said, "Jonathan, you know I never wanted to leave you or your brother. It was always my intention to come back and get y'all. Your dad and I had our differences and I'm sorry that it had to affect you. I know it doesn't seem like it, but living without y'all has been extremely difficult for me," she said. "Don't think that I was just living my life and not thinking about y'all.

"I had been in such a dark place for years. It's hard for me to enjoy life or 'celebrate' holidays because y'all weren't there with me. I'd been battling depression and sickness for such a long time over this. I felt like a failure as a parent and I don't even know if I know how to be a mother," she continued.

"So many people had used my kids against me, including my ex-boyfriend. Every time we got in a disagreement, he would throw not having my kids or abandoning my kids in my face. I don't want to make any excuses for what I've done but I know I've hurt you. I want you to know that I've been hurting as well. I don't know how to make up for lost time," she said. "The reason I don't call is because I'm afraid of what you think of me. You're grown now and at times I feel like there is nothing I can do to undo what's been done."

At this point, my mom and I were both in tears.

"When I did try to reach out to you, your dad wouldn't allow me to. I bought a cellphone and shipped it to your dad's house so we could communicate without your dad, but he wouldn't allow it. I partially quit trying because I didn't want to get you into any trouble with your dad," she explained.

"Jonathan, I had been battling suicide ever since I left you guys. I pray that you can one day find it in your heart to forgive me."

"I know ma, I forgive you. All I ever wanted was a relationship with you. I honestly don't care about you leaving and everything that happened. All I desire is a relationship," I responded.

My heart had completely softened to my mother. I felt such a heavy burden lift off of me. I honestly wasn't thinking about myself at that moment, but my heart was focused on helping my mother. Although I was affected by her leaving me, as her son, I wanted what was best for my mother. I could tell she needed healing. I saw the pain in her eyes. She not only needed spiritual healing but physical healing as well. I needed the love of my mother and she needed the love of her son.

As her son, it was hard for me to watch my mother go through that pain no matter what she did to me. I no longer felt like a victim. I just wanted to see her happy and healed which would be enough to make me happy. A bond between a mother and son can never be broken no matter the time or distance spent separated.

I asked if I could go use the restroom. When I left the restroom, my mom wanted me to see the rest of the remodeling that she did to the house. I can't lie, it looked great, but I was still missing the old childhood look of the house. She told me that she did most of the remodeling herself. I didn't know she was that crafty. She reached out her phone and showed me some of the other things she'd made. I was astonished because I liked to make things myself. I've always been really good with my hands.

She took me into her room and showed me her closet. It was full of shoes, clothes, and all kinds of accessories. She started telling me how much she's into fashion and how she just loves to dress up. I was smiling from ear to ear because I loved fashion myself. I always wondered partially why I am the way that I am. My dad didn't have any of these traits so it was good to see where I got it from. The more my mother and I talked, the more I found out that I was just like her. I was like a little kid in a candy store jumping for joy.

After she got done showing me around, I headed out to the neighborhood party. She told me she would meet me out there later. I caught up with my uncle Bruce and some of his old friends. They were all happy to see me and asked me how I had been since I relocated to Texas.

After conversations with them, I grabbed a bite to eat. I wanted to get some food in my system before I second line danced for the rest of the night.

When I got done, the whole neighborhood was in the street second line dancing all over the neighborhood. When we were all done dancing, I ran into a few of my old childhood friends. Man was I happy to see them! I was always the youngest out of the group, so I know it was different for them to see me all grown up. We laughed and talked about old time stories of our childhood growing up. Life came and went by so fast over the years. Most of them had wives and kids already. They asked me how football was going and said they were proud of me for what I'd accomplished thus far.

They said, "we always knew you'd be the one to make it."

I responded, "I wanted to make it for all of us. I know we all didn't have the opportunity like I did, so whenever I played football I felt like I was playing for all of us."

I saw my mom coming from up the way out of the corner of my eye.

"Tara, you got out of the house?!" one of my friends yelled.

"Yea, my baby is in town so I had to come out of the house," she responded.

We stayed together for the rest of the party.

Everybody was happy to see my mother and me together. It had been 20 plus years since they'd seen it. After I finished mingling with everyone, I drove to the other side of the neighborhood where the levees were. My brother and I used to always play on this hill racing up and down. I remember us taking our first pictures in our rugrats outfit for Halloween. The hill brought back so many memories. Just right over the hill was the Mississippi River. I remember wanting to swim in it when I was younger and my brother rushing to grab me before I jumped in. I walked the trail on the hill for about a mile reminiscing my childhood memories and talking to God.

Truthfully, I was happy to see everybody at the reunion, but I was crushed not seeing my brother there. He was still in jail and I didn't know when or if I'd ever see him again. When I got done, I drove back to my mom's house to meet up with her and my uncle before we went to downtown New Orleans.

Around 12:30 a.m., we went to café du monde to have beignets and coffee. We sat at the table reminiscing and telling stories. It felt good to be around family again. When we got done eating, we walked over to Bourbon Street. If you know anything about New Orleans, Bourbon Street is the place to be if you're looking to party. It wasn't really my scene. It was too congested and people were everywhere. I hate being in places where I really don't know my surroundings. As we walked through Bourbon Street, I felt very uneasy and something inside of me wouldn't let me get comfortable being there. When we left there, we walked over to where the ferries were stationed. I loved the view and my mom wanted to take some pictures of me and her. That was our first photo in more than 20 years. After we finished taking pictures, we went home.

I slept in the next morning. It was my last day in New Orleans and Lord knows I didn't want to leave. I waved goodbye to my aunty and then went over to my mom's to say my goodbyes. I could tell she didn't want me to leave so we went to go get some crawfish. When the cashier gave us the amount to pay, I reached for my wallet to pay but my mom insisted that she would pay. I didn't want her to, but I felt the Holy Spirit telling me to let her. I needed to feel like a child, and she needed to feel like a mother.

When we finished eating, we headed to my grandmother's (my dad's mother) house. She found out I was in town and wanted to see me. I didn't stay long because I had to get back on the road. As we were leaving my mom suggested another place where I could get some food to-go. She knew that I loved fried wings and shrimp fried rice. She was raving about this place so I had to give it a try. Let's just say the food was halfway gone before I left the parking lot. There's not too many places in New Orleans where the food is not up to par. I don't recommend eating and driving but I couldn't help it. We finally got back to my mom's house. We took some more pictures and said our final goodbyes.

I was sad as I drove away. Leaving my mom and my childhood home behind. On the drive back home, I listened to worship music, talked to God and cried. When I finally got to Houston, it dawned on me that it had been 7 years since the day I had last seen my mom. This was nothing but God's doing. Due to so much crying, it didn't take me long to fall asleep. When I went to bed that night, I had the most vivid dream of my brother to date.

When I woke up, I woke up in tears. I suppressed how I felt for my brother for so long that I'd always put it at the back of my mind, but for some reason, God was pulling all of it back up again. Not too long after I got up, I got a phone call from my brother from jail. I was in shock because I just dreamt of him and when I woke up, he was calling my phone. It had been 5 years since we last spoke. My brother had reached out to me several times, but it was hard for me to communicate with him. There were times that I partially blamed myself for him being in jail. I also was angry at my mother as well and felt she was partially at fault too. My brother and I had such a strong bond that when we got separated, it was really hard for me to recover from that. I knew God wouldn't allow me to rest until this was resolved.

My brother and I talked on the phone for over an hour. I tried to apologize to my brother for not communicating with him but he didn't even want an apology. All he wanted was to hear my voice and asked that I check in with him from time to time. He wanted some recent photos of me and some football pictures.

When we got off the phone, I busted into tears again. I was tired of crying and never been much of a crier but I couldn't help it. The love of the Father became so real to me that I couldn't stop crying and He was healing me through my tears. I'd cried over these situations for years and felt like the problems would never end, but God always had a plan and a purpose for why I went through what I went through. It had been a long journey, but I was finally on my road to recovery.

CONFIRMATION

Matt, Donovan and I linked up to start recording a new episode for the podcast. Before we started recording, Matt and Donovan were inquiring about my trip to New Orleans. They knew how important it was for me to rekindle that relationship with my mother. I told them all about it and they were both extremely happy for me. Dominique and I spoke briefly after we were finished recording. He was extremely happy for me as well. He was actually the person that talked me out of not going to New Orleans when I was being apprehensive. It's always good to have someone in your corner that will hold you accountable for what God wants you to do.

After I got off the phone with Dominique, we headed over to Matt's house to watch some college football. Mr. Davis had some food waiting for us when we arrived. We all sat around the living room TV watching the college bowl games. When the games ended, I headed back home. I had to be up early for work the next day. I got to work a few minutes early because I needed to turn my rental car from the trip back in. On my way to work, I stopped by the gas station to fill the car up with gas.

When I got to work, it was a slow morning, so I had some time on my hand. I pulled out my phone and started watching a sermon by Dr. Matthew Stevenson. I had recently discovered him a few months back. He was different from all the other pastors that I'd watched in the past. I found myself watching one video after another over the last couple of months. There was something unique and different about him and his ministry that I was drawn to. I couldn't put my finger on exactly what it was but I knew it was God.

Shortly after, I went out back to go wash a few cars. We were short staffed, so I decided to help out. While I was washing cars, I heard the Holy Spirit whisper "World Changers conference." I didn't know what He was talking about so I brushed it off and continued washing cars. When I finished, I pulled out my phone and started scrolling on Instagram. After about 5 minutes of scrolling, I saw "Sign up for World Changers Summit" on Dr. Matthew Stevenson's page. I thought to myself, "God, do you really want me to attend this event? God if it's you, give me another sign."

I walked back into the building, grabbed my work tablet and started checking customers into their cars. I checked about two or 3 customers into their cars, and I had one more to go before my lunch break. I met a Caucasian man that I spoke with briefly before getting him checked into his car.

"Okay sir, all I need is your driver's license to finish the transaction." I stated.

"Sure, no problem," he responded.

He reached into his pocket to pull out his driver's license. It read Chicago, Illinois.

I thought, "that's strange. This is the first person I've met from Chicago since working at Enterprise. Maybe it's just a coincidence."

After the transaction was completed, I went to the nearby taco truck to grab myself a bite to eat. They had some of the best tacos in all of Houston. They always cooked fresh food right there in front of me. When I got done eating, I clocked back in and started checking customers in. After checking in a few more customers, I ran into another lady that was from the southside of Chicago.

"Well maybe this isn't a coincidence after all," I thought to myself. I finished up the rest of my day before I headed home. By this time, I was used to my long hours. My perspective of working there started changing over time. I started enjoying my interactions with customers more than I previously did. I remember hating having to talk to so many people, but it wasn't as bad as I thought. It forced me out of my comfort zone. The job was teaching me social skills, communication skills, and how to be marketable.

It wasn't my dream job but all of this was working for my good. I was able to even develop meaningful connections with some of my customers. I remember Pastor Johnson coming in to rent frequently. He was a regular and I tried my best to give him as much of a discount as I could. He was a cool old man. Every time he walked in the store, he would ask for me. He wouldn't deal with anyone else but me.

Pastor Johnson came in later that week on a Friday afternoon. He wasn't as energetic as he normally was. I could tell something was wrong. I didn't want to bother asking him about it so I brushed it off. When I got back to my desk, the Holy Spirit kept nudging me to pray for him. I started praying under my breath at work until He stopped me midway and told me to call him. I didn't have his number in my phone, so I got it out of the database.

"Hey Pastor Johnson, this is Jonathan. I just checked you into the car. I hope you don't mind me getting your number from our system."

"Oh no, not at all. What's going on?" He asked.

"I was just wondering if I could pray for you." I responded. "Sure you can." he said.

I closed my eyes and began to pray with him over the phone. When I finished, Pastor Johnson informed me that his wife had been in the hospital for the past few weeks and how he had given up hope. He talked about how tired and exhausted he was seeing his wife in the state that she was in. He told me how much he needed that prayer and how timely it was. When I got off the phone with him, I felt a release and reassurance that I did exactly what the Holy Spirit asked me to do even though I was out of my comfort zone.

The next day I got to work for my weekend shift. It was just my boss Will and I working the Saturday shift. We had our morning meeting and opened up afterwards. Our first customer came in asking if we could give him a ride up the road.

"Sure we can. As long as it's within 5 miles." I stated.

I pulled out my phone and searched the address where he needed to be dropped off. It was only 4 miles away. We both got in the car and started conversing.

"Where are you coming from?" I asked.

"Chicago. I came to Houston to deliver a car." He responded.

We continued the rest of our conversation with small talk. I'd never been much of a morning person, so I was still fighting to wake up. I drove him off and headed back to the office. "Wait. Did he say Chicago?" I asked myself. This was the third person I had met that week from Chicago.

"God, this must be you," I thought to myself. I don't know what God had planned for me in Chicago but I knew I needed to be there even if I went by myself. Luckily, payday was that week so I went ahead and purchased my conference ticket.

CHICAGO

I went to church the following Sunday. I was still trying to find my footing within the church. Matt had been asking me for a while now when I was going to start serving in church. God knows I wanted to, but I just didn't know where to. I had loved church and the ministry but I had a gut feeling that this wasn't the place I needed to be anymore. All of my new friends attended this church and leaving was the last thing I wanted to do.

The pastor and Matt were really close. He was actually his spiritual father. (A spiritual father is someone that is usually the head of a church or someone positioned in authority. They may not be biologically related to you, but they take on the role of a parent. They teach and train you in the ways of God).

Talking to my friends about my problems was great, but I knew I needed something more. I think it's good to have those conversations with your friends, but sometimes friends don't have what it takes to get you over your current situation. Whereas a spiritual father has the capability of pouring into you the revelation of God into your life to point you in the right direction. The church service was good and the pastor taught on financial literacy. God knew that was one area that I needed improvement on. On the drive home, I thought about the possibility of a new church home. Everyone was great, the services were good but I just wasn't connecting anymore and I didn't even know why. I felt like I was eating but I couldn't get full anymore.

Matt called me and we talked briefly about the World Changers Summit. Instead of going by myself, we decided to make it a group trip. The only thing left was to buy my plane ticket. Matt, Falyn and Donovan purchased later that night so they were all expecting to be on the same flight. I on the other hand had waited another week before I purchased my flight so I bought a different flight. We all pitched in on an Airbnb that was about 20 minutes from the convention center. A friend of ours, Chelsea V., decided to join us on the trip. I went shopping to get a few outfits for the summit. I didn't know the dress code but I always liked to be prepared. You never know who you'll meet.

The day finally arrived to go to Chicago and I was really excited to go. I was excited about the event but I also was excited about finally getting to go to Chicago considering that I've never been before. I'd always heard the city was beautiful, diverse and had really great places to eat. I knew something special was waiting on me since God was so adamant about me being there. I finally landed in Chicago. I ordered my uber to pick me up and take me to the Airbnb.

I stepped outside and I was greeted by the gusting winds and freezing cold weather. I see why they call it the "windy city." The others were still on the plane. I got to the Airbnb and couldn't get in because Falyn booked it. I sat outside in the freezing cold with all my luggage. I was just praying someone would let me in the building. Just my luck, the owner of the complex was leaving the building and decided to let me in until the others got there. I waited for about another hour and a half before the others got there. We went upstairs, picked out our separate rooms and headed to the convention center to register. When we arrived we were all given our registration badges for the summit. We drove back to the Airbnb and grabbed a bite to eat. We ate at a famous chinese restaurant and the food was good as advertised. When we finished eating, we made our way back to the convention center.

As we walked inside the line was already wrapping around. We stood in line for about another hour before finally entering into the evening service. We still got some pretty good seats. The worship service was amazing. I had never been in an atmosphere like that before. When worship service was over we ran into some of the church members from the church back in Houston. We also ran into Mojana, a friend of Matt's who I'd met before but only spoke to briefly. She had two of her friends with her Chelsea E. and Billie. We all talked briefly and decided to sit together the following day. We left shortly after and when we returned to the Airbnb, we stayed up for a little while, conversing before we all went to bed.

I woke up the next morning, ordered some McDonalds because I was pressed for time. After eating, I got in the shower and got dressed. I brought a salmon suit and a black turtleneck to go with it. The others had on street clothes but I decided to stay dressed up. There's no such thing as overdressed in my mind. We all loaded up into the uber and headed to the convention. When we walked in, they were already praying and you could feel a strong presence of God in the auditorium. The first two speakers spoke before we had an intermission. During intermission, I grabbed a bite to eat but I had to make it quick because I had a deliverance session next.

The deliverance room was just around the corner from the auditorium. Donovan and I walked in together.

Donovan whispered, "man, you feel that?"

I responded, "yes I do. I thought it was just me."

We were the first two in the room, but since we knew each other, they made us sit separately. Not too long after, the room filled up. We were all given instructions on what deliverance was and its importance. After reading the prompt, the woman reading began to pray and the rest of the workers spread out across the room and began praying for people. As she prayed, I heard screams like I never heard before. I heard the torment of so many souls in the room. When the people walked in they looked normal, but as prayer was being ministered, the agony of the tormented souls began to cry out. The only way I can describe it was like hearing hell on earth. I'd never been a part of anything like that before or seen it in person. I tried not to focus on everything else going on in the room but it was hard for me not to.

About 20 minutes in, almost everybody had been prayed for except me. Then finally a woman came up and started praying for me. She began to tell me all about my life and all that I'd been through including the trauma. She informed me that God wanted to free me completely and she continued to pray for me. About another 15 minutes went by and the screams were even louder than before. When it was all over, I made eye contact with another worker and she pointed to me and told me to come talk to her.

I walked over to her and she spoke to me saying, "you are a seer, a prophet of God. Ever since you were a child, you've always had kingly dreams and visions. You've always thought you were strange and weird because of it. Sometimes you try to hide it, but God is raising you up. Don't be afraid to talk about the things God has shown you. There will be a time where God allows you to share the revelations He's given you."

I stood there with a shocked look on my face. How can a woman I just met tell me about the secrets God had shown me without me ever telling her. I knew this had to be God. I headed back to the auditorium where everyone was and I couldn't stop thinking about what just happened. My mind was still blown away. We listened to a couple other speakers before they dismissed us for dinner.

We caught up with Mojana, Chelsea E. and Billie. Chelsea E. and Billie went to eat somewhere else and the rest of us went to Sharks. This restaurant was suggested by a few of the local residents so we decided to try it out. It was nothing short of spectacular. I enjoyed every bit of it. We sat and talked about the conference. Matt, Donovan and I talked about the deliverance service. We had a real humorous moment when Donovan said someone prayed and laid hands on him and didn't realize he was laid out on the floor for about 5 minutes until he got up. I told them briefly about what had happened to me and how that lady ministered to me secretive things that only God and I knew about.

After sharing my story, we headed back to the convention center for the evening session with Dr. Matthew Stevenson. He was the closing speaker for that night and I couldn't wait to finally hear him in person. We all linked back up in the auditorium and sat together. Shortly after praise and worship, Dr. Stevenson walked on stage in one of the flyest suits I'd ever seen. I thought to myself, "where can I get one of those?"

When he grabbed the mic, he had a group of his male leaders come out on stage and they all had on different colors of his suit design. He informed us that he was releasing a clothing line. Shortly after, he began preaching. He was very intellectual and spoke with a lot of authority. It was a big difference between watching him on screen and seeing him live in person. I'm not sure what it was about him and his ministry, but I felt very connected to it. On the way back to the Airbnb, we stopped to get a bite to eat. The last thing on the list to try was some deep dish pizza. We talked for a little while about how phenomenal the service was before heading back to the Airbnb. Everybody was exhausted. It had been a long day. We didn't stay up late like we normally would. We all went to bed pretty early considering it would be another long day with flights to catch in the afternoon right after the summit.

Each of us woke up early the next day and packed our bags before we headed to the convention center. When we walked in we sat next to Mojana, Chelsea E. and Billie. They had our seats saved. Dr. Stevenson opened the morning sessions after worship. After him, a few other speakers spoke. They were all phenomenal. By the end of it, I had a notebook full of notes. I only had one more session to attend and that was the prophetic session. I walked in and we were all assigned to individual people. They insisted that we pull our phones out to record. The woman that was assigned to me began to prophesy over my life.

> *"Okay Jonathan what I hear for you is you know exactly why you are here. You had the confirmation of why you were supposed to be here before you got here. You've been set apart since you were a child. You've always been sensitive to the things of the spirit. You have real king visions and dreams that are really pertinent to your life. You know things ahead of time and wasn't really sure how you were going to use the information or why it mattered. God says I have put you on this track, I've set you apart, and I'm going to use you for greater things beyond your imagination.*

"You never really fit in with your friends and you've learned to have almost a jokester personality to kind of just blend, but God has set you apart on purpose and intentionally. He's bringing to you the friends necessary to keep going for your future, so you're going to start to see a separation with that. Allow God to do what He has to do to set you apart from those people because they're not going to understand what He's about to do in your life.

"I see God placing His hand over you and you're going to start to see God placing His hand in all things around you. You're going to experience some tough times because you're separated from the things that you were once comfortable with. You are about to be in a season of uncomfortability, because He has to show you how He's created you.

"You begin to build a personality of who you thought you were and what works for you that kind of keeps you out of the spotlight. God says, it is not so, that is not what I called you to be. I have more for you greater than you thought could possibly happen. The call is so great on your life that it's going to be bigger than what you dreamed or imagined. You have glimpses of your future and you question it because you're not sure if it's something that you're able to do.

God says you're going to do it with Me. It is My Spirit that is going to give you the direction and guidance so continue walking forth. Even in that season that God has been dealing with your heart about past pains that you've experienced, because you thought that the things that you experienced shouldn't have happened to you, it was unfair, and if this is what the calling is going to look like then you don't want to do it. God says allow Him to heal your heart in that trauma so that you're able to be whole as you walk into this, because man didn't call you, God did. You're not going to get the affirmation and confirmation that you've been searching for, it is going to come directly from Him.

"Don't be discouraged because God still has a team for you that is going to be able to affirm you and pull out those different gifts and talents that are hidden in you. There is so much talent in you and it seems that you hide it because you don't want to explain it to other people. You don't want to have to explain to them why you are how you are. Why you just get it and they don't. But God says that I have placed that gift inside of you and I am uncovering so that it can be used for my glory.

"Allow God to use you in the way that He desires to. There was a different surrender that you experienced this weekend where you were just like God okay fine, if we're going to do it together let's do it together. God says I am walking with you, I have created a path for you, and I've gone before you. Trust me with this, trust me with this, when things start to look dark and bleak, trust that I am in control. God says that this is what He has for you and don't question Me again, don't question Me again."

After I received that word, I was even more amazed than I was before. I left feeling an overwhelming sense of peace that filled my heart. Knowing that God cared about me more than I could ever imagine, made me feel love like I'd never felt before. These weren't just words of affirmation but they were prophetic. It was the exact word from God that I needed for that exact moment and season of my life. I left that room and conference knowing who I was and my identity in Christ. Not just who I thought I was but who He created me to be.

HOLY SPIRIT

Chicago was an incredible experience and little did I know that life would never be the same after.

I got back to Houston Saturday night, and I was still in awe of everything that happened in Chicago. I was even more excited about the unfolding of God's spoken word over my life. I didn't know exactly how things were gonna play out. I decided I would just surrender the outcome to God, and let him put the puzzle together. For some strange reason I felt things were just getting started in my life, and things were getting ready to be changed forever. I woke up the next morning excited about attending church. It's easy to fall in the habit of making church a routine, and drowning in the formalities of it all. When I got to church I greeted a few of my friends, and headed to the front to find a seat before service began.

Praise and worship was amazing as usual, and the pastor preached a phenomenal message. While driving home I still was trying to find my footing in the church, but I was still feeling a pull in a different direction. I've always been weary of just up and leaving church, because of my personal views or preferences. I wanted to make sure it was God and not me. I also didn't know exactly where I would go. Few days went by and I was still contemplating on visiting another church. On Wednesday of that week I was reminded of a church that was nearby that I had previously visited for a young adult gathering. I decided to check out their church website. Lo and behold they were having bible study that Wednesday night at 7:30 p.m. I thought to myself, "why not give it a try?"

I asked my manager if I could get off a few minutes early so I could go home and freshen up before I go. After showering and getting myself together I headed over to the Wednesday night service. I got there a little early so there weren't too many people in the church. The few members that were there made sure they spoke to me briefly before I sat down. A few more members came in after. I waved hello to each of them as they came in, and they all greeted me with love.

While gazing off to the left side of the room, I suddenly felt a strong presence of God on the right side of the church. I glanced over to my right and saw that a man had just walked into the room. I could literally feel the tangible presence of God all over him. I could literally feel God walking with him as he maneuvered around the room. I had never felt anything like that before in my life. While gazing in that direction I heard the Holy Spirit say this is your Spiritual Father. Now I didn't know this man from Adam, and neither did I know if he was the pastor of the church or not. Also we have never spoken before, but for some reason I felt an instant connection to him.

After he set down, the Bible study had started. I thought maybe he's the pastor, but he wasn't teaching the Bible study like most pastors do. I contemplated on the way that I would introduce myself after church. I knew I heard clearly that he was my spiritual father, but I didn't know exactly how to approach him about it. After the Bible study ended I was headed over to talk to him, but he was busy talking to a few other members so I decided I would catch him next time. I got in the car to drive off, but before I could leave the parking lot the Holy Spirit wouldn't let me leave without talking to him. I got out of my car and headed back inside, he was finishing up a conversation when I approached him.

"Hey, sir it's so nice to meet you. My name is Jonathan Davis."

"I'm Apostle Eminent Tony Irvin. It's nice to meet you, young man. What can I do for you?" he asked.

"I've been struggling with fear and anxiety. I'm in need of prayer." I responded.

He didn't waste any time and started praying for me immediately. When he got done praying he asked me what church I attended, and he said "I can see you're a strong prophet of God, and you need to be around other prophetic people. You want to be in a place where you're being watered so you can grow."

I knew there was more he wanted to tell me by the look on his face, but for whatever reason he didn't. I also noticed that he didn't ask me to join his church. He was integral enough to allow me to make that decision on my own. I left that night knowing this was most likely the place God wanted me to be. It was still gonna take more convincing to steer me away from the other church. I decided I would visit the church for Sunday service to see what it was like. I was desperately hungry to have a deeper relationship with God. I was willing to do whatever it took to get there by any means necessary. I was willing to let go of any and everything to find Him. Sunday came around, and it was finally time for me to visit the church. I walked in and was ushered to the back row of the church to take my seat. Praise and worship started, and I noticed a difference from the church I was currently attending.

They didn't just sing songs they planned to sing, but their songs were Prophetically led by the Holy Spirit. The songs were being created as they ministered in the service. The atmosphere was very unique and different. Shortly after Apostle Eminent walked in, and I could still feel the presence of God on him as he entered the room. I asked the Holy Spirit, "why is your presence so strong on his life?" He revealed to me that he was a man that lived in the secret place (see Psalm 91). The Holy Spirit revealed to me that he spent so much time with God that he began carrying his presence.

After worship he began to pray, and you could feel the Holy Spirit taking over the service, and unlike most churches the order of service was led by the spirit. Apostle began prophesying and stated that God wanted to grow someone in the prophetic, and that it was time to grow in that gifting! He didn't say my name specifically, but I knew that word was for me. As he continued to speak he began to prophesy everything that I dreamt about the night before church, and every instruction God had given me that I wrote down in my Journal. Apostle asked if there's anything that anyone wanted to share that God was putting on their heart. I could feel God nudging me to go up there, but I was extremely nervous.

A few of the members stood up and began to prophesy. You could tell that most of them were trained and groomed in the prophetic. On the other hand, I wasn't trained yet and it made me even more nervous. I could still feel God tugging on me to go up and speak. I finally got the courage and made my way down to the front of the church. I was handed the microphone, and my heart was beating out of my chest. I could hardly get my words out. I got a few sentences out, and stopped mid sentence. When I was done, Apostle laid his hands on my forehead, and I felt the Spirit of God go throughout my body. I felt the electricity going all through my body as I was laid out on the floor. I had never experienced anything like this before. I tried to get up, but I couldn't. The weight of God's Glory was on me so strong I couldn't move. I was baptized by the fire of the Holy Spirit that night (see Matthew 3:11).

I'd seen it on tv and read about it in scripture, but never did I think I would encounter the Holy Spirit the way I did. When you are baptized with Fire of the Holy Spirit you will know it when it happens!

When I got home that night I was still feeling the same electricity flowing throughout my body. It was hard for me to sleep that night, because I was still drenched in His Glory and the Holy Spirit radiating throughout my body. I could feel his presence all over my house and in my bedroom. I knew that touch had changed me forever. There was an immediate transfer of Grace that came upon me that night.

The Person of the Holy Spirit became more real to me than life itself. I didn't understand the totality of who the Holy Spirit was until I encountered Him. I found out that He wasn't just a dove floating around, but that He is an actual person. He is the third person of the trinity. He is the one that God sent to help aid us in this life. In John 14:15-20 it states, *"If you love me, keep my commands. And I will ask the Father, and He will give you another advocate to help you and be with you forever, the Spirit of truth. The world cannot accept him, because it neither sees Him nor knows Him. But you know Him, for He lives with you and will be in you. I will not leave you as orphans; I will come to you. Before long, the world will not see me anymore, but you will see me. Because I live, you also will live."* In scripture Jesus clearly lets us know that He was going back to the Father, and He was sending the Holy Spirit in His place.

The scriptures also let us know that many won't receive Him, because they can't physically see Him. If you were like me, many of us hardly knew who the Holy Spirit was. It was all about Jesus, the Father, and the importance of the Holy Spirit was undermined. The Holy Spirit is essential in the everyday life of the believer. Jesus is now seated at the right hand of the father, and the Holy Spirit is here to aid us in this life. Jesus, the Father, and the Holy Spirit are one. We cannot get to the Father without Jesus, and we cannot truly know Jesus without the help of the Holy Spirit. The Holy Spirit comforts, guides, counsels, and everything He does points us to Jesus. Jesus in return leads us to the father.

I was finally able to get some sleep that night, but when I got up that morning it started all over again. I could feel the electricity flowing all throughout my body. I could feel it all up and through my bones. I couldn't help but think about what happened to me, and if this feeling was ever going to go away. When I got to work that morning it finally dawned on me just how quickly everything changed since leaving Chicago. I went back and listened to the prophetic recording that I received from the lady at the summit. In less than a week, 80% of it had already come to pass. I found a new church home, community, met my spiritual father, and received the baptism of the Holy Spirit.

While at work I was still feeling the strong sensation throughout my body and it was only getting stronger. I asked God if He could ease up, because it was very overwhelming. I thought to myself, "how could someone even function every day like this?"

I got home that night and was still trying to wrap my mind around everything that was going on. I didn't know exactly who to talk to about what was happening to me, and didn't want anyone to think that I was going crazy. After watching a few college football games, I went to my room to get ready for bed. While I was dozing off I could literally feel the

Holy Spirit tugging on me wanting me to stay up and fellowship with him. The only way I could describe it is like when a newborn baby crawls on top of a parent wanting to have intimacy, stay up, and play at 3 am in the morning. I tried to shake it off but He just wouldn't leave me alone.

Eventually, I got out of bed and fellowshipped with Him for the rest of the night. I messaged the Apostle that following afternoon to see if he could help further explain what was going on with me. He told me to give him a call when I got off work. When I got on the phone with him he insisted that I read *Good Morning Holy Spirit* by Benny Hinn. Apostle insisted that I would get a better understanding of everything after I read it.

After we got off the phone I downloaded the book on my kindle. Let's just say after about 10min of reading I was glued to the book. I couldn't put the book down. I stayed up all night reading. In the book Benny Hinn talked about his personal encounter with the Holy Spirit, and how it changed his entire life. Reading that book blessed me tremendously. Benny and my experiences were very similar, and yet uniquely different. It was refreshing to know that there was someone I could relate to with a similar story as mine.

While at work the next day Mojana, Chelsea, and I spoke briefly about everything that had been happening to me since Chicago. The three of us had gotten extremely close within a matter of days after leaving the conference. We would stay up on the phone for hours talking about God. I couldn't help but share with them my experience with the Holy Spirit. We were all amazed at just how fast things were happening in our lives. I remember one day being on the phone with them for 11hrs straight fellowshipping together. After a long day at work, I found myself drifting off to sleep around 2 a.m.

Little did I know that the slumber would be abruptly interrupted, as I jolted awake with my heart pounding in my chest.

Glancing at the clock, I discovered that it was already 9 a.m. The idea of returning to sleep was out of the question after the out-of-body experience I had just encountered. The vividness of it all left me startled.

It wasn't merely a vision; it felt more real than anything I had ever known. Every sense was heightened in that ethereal realm—I could feel, touch, taste, and smell as if I were firmly grounded on earth. Emotions coursed through me with an intensity beyond imagination. As I rested my head on the pillow, preparing to sleep, an unexplainable occurrence unfolded. In the blink of an eye, I found myself standing in a long, winding line, surrounded by countless individuals ahead and behind me. It became clear that this was a place of judgment.

Before me stood a stage, upon which God was seated on a majestic throne. Though His face and body were veiled from my sight, a radiant light emanated from His presence. The sheer power and magnitude that emanated from Him overwhelmed me, filling me with a gripping fear that defies description. Every word He spoke reverberated through the air like thunder, resonating with unimaginable authority.

As I surveyed the scene, I noticed smaller thrones positioned on the stage, occupied by individuals I couldn't quite discern. They appeared to be elders or figures of great importance. Taking in my surroundings, I realized I was in a waiting room, reminiscent of an earthly courtroom but on an enormous scale. The room teemed with angels, celestial beings, and individuals summoned for judgment. It struck me that this waiting room existed just beyond the gates of heaven—a space where the final reckoning took place before one could enter the city. I will reveal more details about this extraordinary setting later.

Though still far from the stage, I sensed myself gradually drawing closer, as if was being carried on an invisible elevator. I moved without my feet touching the ground, defying the laws that govern the earthly realm. The experience was truly remarkable.

Before my eyes, a man stood before God, a renowned musician from my earthly life. Though I couldn't hear their conversation, I did witness the outcome of his judgment. The man received a magnificent white robe and joined the heavenly choir of angels on the left side of the throne. The sheer beauty and the celestial melodies that resonated from this angelic ensemble were beyond compare. Behind them, was a huge arched doorway that only those who made it passed judgment could enter.

As I continued to stand in line, nervousness and overwhelming emotions washed over me I couldn't help but reflect upon the wrongs I had committed throughout my lifetime. With each step forward, I knew there was no escape from facing my own judgment. In the blink of an eye, my turn arrived, and God summoned me to the stage. As I approached, He directed me to stand in front of myself—a notion that seemed inexplicable. Yet, it was as if God addressed each thought as it arose within me, communicating with me telepathically, bypassing the need for spoken words.

To my astonishment, I stood face to face with my own spirit, as if gazing into a mirror. The realization dawned upon me—there was another "me" standing before me, distinct yet interconnected. My spirit, separate from my physical being, bore witness against me, testifying with intimate knowledge of my life that I had long forgotten or suppressed. My Spirit possessed a comprehensive understanding of every event, every moment, and the intricate details surrounding them. My spirit held the complete record of my existence since the day I was born, and it was now revealing it all. I stood there, utterly shocked. God required no words from me, for my spirit provided Him with all the necessary information. According to

Proverbs 20:27, the human spirit serves as the lamp of the Lord, shedding light upon the depths of one's being. It was this lamp that God used to search the recesses of my soul.

Imagine yourself in a courtroom, where the judge summons a witness to the stand, only to find that the witness is none other than yourself. It was a profound mystery to me, witnessing how God used my own being to judge me. I want to emphasize once again that my thoughts were audible to God, enabling Him to hear my innermost musings without the need for spoken words. Neither my spirit nor God nor any of the celestial beings moved their lips to communicate. Instead, a telepathic exchange occurred, where the language of thought carried a sound that resonated without any bodily movements.

Shortly after in front of me, a portal materialized, revealing a panoramic display of my life—past, present, and future—all unfolding like a living tapestry. It resembled a projection screen, yet it possessed an inexplicable vitality. Through this timeless portal, God showcased the entirety of my existence—the good, the bad, and the ugly.

I witnessed pivotal moments, particularly those where a mentor figure, Pastor Bell, consistently urged me to obey God's call on my life. I could remember every conversation with Pastor Bell revolved around obeying God. At the time, I remained unaware that God utilized him as a vessel, imparting the principle of obedience into me. Pastor Bell's words echoed God's own instructions. I stood there speechless with an overwhelming conviction, realizing I had no valid excuses or room for deceit. You see in that spiritual realm, where all was laid bare, my spirit ensured the transparency necessary for the testimony. The lord allowed me to see what he was seeing as he was searching my spirit. It was as if he let me into his mind. Just as you use a search engine to find what you seek, my spirit served as God's search engine, combing through my existence.

Before finalizing my judgment, God permitted me to witness the judgment of another individual. In an instant, I found myself transported to a church building, observing a young man who served as a drummer in that local congregation. In the absence of the pastor, the First Lady requested the young man to play the drums. Astonishingly, he responded by mocking and laughing at her, joined by his friends. I witnessed this scene unfold in real-time, as if I were physically present. God's disappointment at this man's refusal to serve his leader and the church was evident. However, I was not privy to the ultimate fate awaiting this individual. God allowed me to see his mistake, because he wanted me to see how important serving is to his Heart.

In Philippians we see Jesus himself take on the role of a servant. "In your relationships with one another, have the same mindset as Christ Jesus Who, being in very nature God, did not consider equality with God something to be used to his own advantage; rather, he made himself nothing by taking the very nature of a SERVANT, being made in human likeness and being found in appearance as a man he humbled himself by becoming OBEDIENT to death, even death on a cross! (Philippians 2:5-8 NIV)

Returning to the courtroom, my thoughts immediately gravitated toward my struggle with pornography—the sin that haunted me most during my earthly life. However, to my surprise, God disregarded those thoughts. He was well aware of them; in fact, I could feel him listening to them. Here I am again standing in front of God, and the next words spoken to me was "why haven't you been obedient, and why haven't you been serving?" (See 1 Samuel 15:22). Immediately I was back in my body awakening from this extraordinary encounter.

On that day, an overwhelming sense of the Fear of God came over me. It ignited a deep reverence within me that permeated every aspect of my life. I came to a profound realization that God possesses ultimate authority and reigns sovereign over all. It doesn't matter how big, small, or great you are we all will give an account for our time spent on earth. No one will escape the Judgment seat of Christ.

Romans 14:12 states that all men shall give an account of himself to God. Sadly, there are many that believe that by not believing in God that can escape his judgment. I'm here to tell you do not deceive yourself.

As I stood among countless others in a line, awaiting our individual judgments, I couldn't help but ponder how I could be in a room with multitudes of people, yet feel so alone and isolated. Listen, there are no safety rails in heaven; you won't have anything to lean on to give you a sense of comfort. You won't have anyone there that you can confide in to give you a sense of peace. No one will be there to hold you by the hand. When you come to the end of your journey on earth, it will just be you and God.

Just as it was in the beginning so shall it be in the end. The topic of judgment encompasses various doctrinal beliefs, each offering its perspective on how it will unfold. Prior to my encounter, I, too, held personal beliefs, but this experience provided a glimpse into the true nature of how judgment will be when we stand before God. When you stand in that light everything is exposed. Nothing is hidden for the eyes of the lord is everywhere. Every document detailing your life is recorded within in your spirit and God will use you to judge you. Your spirit will be on the witness stand!

Let us reflect upon Romans 8:16, where it is written, "The Spirit itself beareth witness with our spirit that we are the children of God." Here, the term "witness" refers to an individual summoned to court to provide testimony in a case. The responses given by a witness in court are regarded as evidence. Prior to testifying, a witness solemnly promises to speak the truth.

Consider this: when we stand before God, our innermost being, our spirit, acts as the bearer of witness on behalf of God. Within our spirit resides a comprehensive collection of intricate documents, meticulously recording the entirety of our lives. I refer to this aspect of our being as the PERFECT WITNESS.

In the presence of God, our spirit unveils the evidence it carries, testifying to the truth of our actions, thoughts, and intentions. This intimate connection between our spirit and God's divine wisdom ensures a just and impartial judgment. It is a moment where the depths of our being are laid bare, and the truth is revealed with utmost clarity.

This awakening also brought about a liberation from the fear of man which was something that I was struggling with as of late. It became evident to me that titles and social status hold no significance when facing judgment. Every one of us, regardless of our position or background, must endure the same scrutiny and be accountable for our time spent here on Earth (see Romans 14:12) These truths resonated with the story of Exodus, where God orchestrated a plan to free the Israelites from Egyptian captivity. Moses, the vessel chosen by God, experienced a life-altering encounter in the wilderness at the burning bush.

Moses, though raised within Pharaoh's household, had been brought up as an Egyptian, disconnected from his Hebrew heritage. Moses was immersed in Egyptian culture, traditions, and pagan worship, he had yet to shed the fear of man. Therefore, when God revealed Himself to Moses, He did so in a way that shattered any remnants of human fear. This was essential because Moses was about to confront Pharaoh, the most powerful figure in all of Egypt. It is a recurring theme throughout Scripture that God instills the fear of God in individuals before their rise to prominence. "The fear of the Lord is the beginning of knowledge, but fools despise wisdom" (Proverbs 1:7 NKJV). We see this same principle applied in the life of Paul while on the road to Damascus (Acts 9). We also see this in the life of Isaiah when he was caught up to the throne room of God (Isaiah 6).

The fear of God is essential fuel that propels our spiritual journey, an indispensable asset for believers. Without it, we are incomplete, unable to function as we were intended. It stands as the foundational cornerstone of wisdom (Proverbs 9). Embracing the fear of God becomes one of the driving forces in our lives, it's an unwavering guide that propels us toward purity of heart. It is through this fear, residing deep within our hearts and subconscious minds, that we maintain a constant state of awareness of God's presence, grounding us in our journey with the Lord.

NEW WINE

After my third time visiting God Encounter Church, I became a member. I finally came to terms with the fact that this was the place God wanted me to be. Everything about my life was changing since I was connected to this ministry. I learned that no man rises on his own. The oil that was being poured into my life was in the hand of my spiritual father.

It's not that he was replacing God in my life but God wanted to teach me how to serve and obey. Elisha was a student of Elijah and Samuel was a student of Eli. They both became powerful men of God, but they had to learn how to serve. Each of these students were assigned by God to their teachers and just like they were — so was I. It's easy to go out and pick anyone to be your spiritual parent, but we must ask ourselves, "is this person assigned by God for my life?"

Although that person may have a great ministry, that flourishing does not mean that person is chosen by God to raise you up in ministry. Apostle Eminent's life carried the oil specifically tailored for me by God. This is why God placed me there under his leadership. Every time he got up to preach, I could feel the oil in his life being poured into me. These impartations (giving and receiving of spiritual gifts, blessings, healing, baptism in the Holy Spirit, etc., for the work of the ministry; the transference of these 'gifts' from one man or woman of God to another), grew stronger overtime.

Apostle and I would speak briefly over the phone, and he would never take credit for anything. He would always give credit to God for everything. He is truly the meekest man I have ever met. I truly believe that God's greatest leaders have yet to be revealed, but God has them hidden until it's time for them to be revealed.

As a believer I've learned not to look for the applause of men and to be known by them, but rather seek to be known in heaven. My spiritual father is a hidden man but he is well known in the spirit. Mojana, Chelsea, and I continued to talk frequently about everything that was going on in our lives.

Mojana and I grew even closer over time. Things started to change in our relationship quickly. I know longer wanted to just be friends, but I could see myself having a life long partnership with her. I wanted to consult God about it before I made any rational decisions on my own. After all there are many good Christian women out there, but that does not mean they are the right one for me. I wasn't just looking for a Christian woman; I needed a woman that was compatible to me.

After I consulted God about my decision I dropped a bug in Mojana's ear. We were already both on the same page so it didn't catch her by surprise. We hadn't seen each other since the conference so we decided that she would fly out from Chicago so we could hangout. When she flew in, I already had my mind set on asking her out. I went to the store to pick her up a gift for traveling to come see me. I made reservations at a restaurant for dinner. While at dinner we had an amazing time, and I was finally able to ask her out. We finally made it official at dinner. It was such a blessing finally meeting the woman of my dreams. Things were moving fast in my life ever since I got to Houston.

It was moving even faster since I last left Chicago. It seemed like every day something new was happening in my life. I had to learn that this was the pace that God had me at in my life. Things were moving very fast but this was my new normal. After the weekend was over, Mojana flew back to Chicago. She was studying for her MCAT. While we were separated, I continued to pray and ask God if she was my wife or not. One day while I was in prayer, I saw a glimpse of Mojana and I in a heavenly place before God with a white cord wrapped around our hands.

This vision painted a picture of marriage ordained by God. I knew after seeing this that she was predestined to be my wife.

While Mojana was in Chicago, she introduced me to a friend of hers named Kenny Agoro. Mojana invited her to God Encounter Church. We sat next to each other at church and chatted for about 45 minutes afterwards. After talking with her, I could tell she was another divine connection. I called Mojana after church and told her how awesome her friend was. A few days later, Kenny introduced us to the Academy of Prophets and Seers (APS) founded by Prophetess A.

APS consists of young prophets and seers. There is a built-in course that is required prior to joining the company. The course breaks down the prophetic and the office of the prophet. It consists of studying the major and minor prophets in the Bible, discovering how we operate individually and finding our identity as a prophet. You don't become a prophet, but you're born a prophet at birth.

"Before I formed you in the womb I knew you, before you were born I set you apart: I appointed you as a prophet to the nations" (Jeremiah 1:5 NIV). A prophet is a person who speaks for God. God's mouthpiece on the earth. "Indeed, the sovereign Lord never does anything until He reveals His plans to His servants the prophets" (Amos 3:7 NLT).

I knew this was something I needed to be apart after discovering that I was a prophet. It was also refreshing to be around a community that understood me, and I could fully be myself. It gave me the comfort ability to be more transparent. I didn't have to feel wired or shameful about what God was doing in my life. I was very hesitant at first to take the course. I didn't want to jump the gun and get ahead of God. I wanted to make sure my decision is what God wanted. Eventually I ended up joining and still to this day, it is one of the best decisions that I have ever made. There is something special that always happens when you get around the right people in the right environment.

It doesn't take long for you to mature and grow. It didn't take long for God to surround me around a community of believers just like me. I'd always felt different and it was fulfilling to be around people who were also different too and understood the things that I'd experienced in the Spirit. I couldn't help but think about the prophecy the woman spoke over my life in Chicago and how 90% of it had already come to pass within a matter of weeks. I met my spiritual father, new church home, community, and soon to be wife. It just solidified how important going to Chicago was for me.

Prior to going to Chicago I had a dream of a roadmap. In the dream I was traveling in a car picking up and dropping off cargo. I traveled from New Orleans to Dallas-Ft.Worth to Houston and my last stop was Chicago. The dream was very detailed of my life's journey. The dream was very specific as it pertained to me gaining and losing cargo. In reality, I was growing spiritually and losing who I used to be. Chicago was the last stop in my dream which was symbolic of getting to the last checkpoint before I continued on my journey.

I finally understood why God was so adamant about me going. My trip to Chicago was the launching pad God used to propel me into my destiny. Being at the right place at the right time is so important. It taught me to walk stride for stride with God. It's important never to get ahead or lag behind him, but instead live in constant obedience.

SPIRITUAL SPRINTER

My relationship with the Holy Spirit continued to grow. I fellowshipped with Him daily. I enjoyed getting to know Him. I would feel His presence all around me continuously. Even while at work, I could feel

Him accompanying me. One day at work, Jordan (my coworker) and I

were fellowshipping in the car.

While we were in the car talking about the Holy Spirit, Jordan stopped mid-sentence, "bro do you feel that?" As his hands shook uncontrollably.

"Yes, I can feel it. It's the Holy Spirit. He's here in the car." I responded. "See I tried to tell you, He's real."

When we got back to Enterprise I had to make a quick run up the street to pick up a gray minivan from one of our local dealerships. When I got to the dealership I located the minivan and proceeded to drive it back. While driving, I started to talk to the Holy Spirit again within my heart. I asked him to reveal himself to me again.

To be honest I did not think anything would come of it, but boy was I wrong. After about 15 minutes I pulled back into the parking lot of the store, and reverse-parked the van back into the parking space. The moment I stopped the car the passenger door swung open, and closed on its own. I sat paralyzed in my seat. I yelled out whoa! Did anyone see that, but there was no one in the back of the store to witness it.

I spoke nothing of this, because I truly believed no one would believe me. However, I couldn't stop thinking about it. When I got home that night after work, I could still feel this overwhelming presence with me. God was truly making himself known to me. If you think that was something what I'm about to share with you next was even more shocking.

As I drifted off to sleep around 10 p.m., a vivid night vision took hold. I found myself observing, myself lying in bed just as I had fallen asleep. To my astonishment, Jesus stood at the foot of my bed, His face veiled from my view. Yet, an overwhelming sense of His presence and unconditional love emanated from Him, penetrating the very core of my being. It is important to note that when Jesus reveals Himself, He chooses the extent of His glory to unveil to each individual.

We may stand in His presence and still not grasp the entirety of His magnificence or comprehend all that He wishes to convey. This remains a captivating mystery to me. In the vision, Jesus departed from my house, leaving the door wide open. I awoke in my bed, feeling a cool breeze wafting through my home. Glancing at the clock, I noticed it was 2:00

a.m. Startled, I pondered how the door could be open. Living alone, I was meticulous about securing my locks each night. I gingerly stepped out of bed, made my way down the hall only to find my door wide open. I peeked outside to see if anyone was outside my door, and there was no one in sight. Despite the many miraculous signs I had already witnessed, unbelief still lingered within my heart. Yet, by the unwavering grace and mercy of God, He persisted in making Himself known to me, even in the face of my wavering faith.

It was in those defining moments that I truly grasped the reality of my experiences. Jesus was undeniably real, and the Holy Spirit had become my constant companion. The words of Psalm 51:11 resonated deeply within me, as I understood the significance of not wanting the Spirit to depart from me. I do not want to do anything to Grieve the Holy Spirit.

Once you have experienced the presence of God as I did, life becomes incomprehensible without it. We are not designed to navigate this journey without the Holy Spirit by our side. Although I cherished my friendships, I found myself seeking solace in conversing with him alone daily.

As the weeks went on I continued to receive revelatory downloads from God. I dove deeper into the Word of God and He met me at my seek level. The more I sought Him, the more He would pour into me. I had several more dreams, visions and encounters but there's one more that I'd like to share.

In this particular dream I was back home attending a party. At the party I saw many of my old friends, family, and people that I looked up to in the past. While talking to one of my friends I saw a man walk into the room. He had on the latest fashion. He was dressed in the finest garments from head to toe. From jewelry, shoes, clothes, he had it all. I could tell that everyone in the room was checking him out.

While standing in the middle of the room, I was able to look out the building as if I was looking through glass. I saw a missile being launched across the city. I knew in the dream that the missile fired was going to cause another missile to be fired back in the same direction that it came from. I noticed that I was the only one that was seeing all of this take place. I was the only one that could see the pending danger. I desperately tried to warn everyone but my words fell on deaf ears. Instead, they continued to party.

Moments later, missiles were launched toward us. One of them struck the base of the building we were in, propelling everything into the air in slow motion. Suspended in mid-air, I observed flames emerging from beneath the earth's surface, steadily rising. As I descended in slow motion, I hit the ground running, clutching a Book in my hand. The only thought on my mind was to proclaim the impending arrival of Jesus. I rushed into a nearby school building, shouting at the top of my lungs, desperately trying to alert them to the dangers outside. They all looked at me like they saw a ghost.

When I noticed that they were not going to pay any attention to me, I moved on to a nearby classroom to warn others. As I entered the classroom, I began to tell the professor about the chaos that was going on outside and that Jesus was coming soon. To my surprise, the professor retrieved a box and began distributing guns to the students. I tried to warn him that weapons wouldn't ensure their safety or quench the blazing fire outside. However, he persisted in distributing firearms, and disregarding my warnings. The truth was, only Jesus had the power to save them from the fire.

I awoke in my bed at 3 a.m., drenched in sweat and tears streaming down my face. My heart ached, and God allowed me to share in the pain

He felt for His people. I was immediately driven to repentance, falling to the floor and weeping for hours. I could feel God's sorrow, and my spirit was grieved. His arrival had caught everyone off guard. He came like a thief in the night. People were consumed by their own desires, distracted by the allure of the latest fashion trends, wealth, cars, and luxurious lifestyles.

They had become blind to the reality unfolding around them. Jesus had attempted to warn them, but no one wanted to listen. In my dream, the professor symbolized a shepherd chosen by God to lead his flock. Instead of conveying the truth, he led them astray, driven by his own evil desires.

The Holy Spirit revealed to me that this represented pastors, and leaders in the church who misused the Word of God for personal gain. They manipulated God's people, distorting scripture to divert them from the truth. Some were messengers of Satan, while others succumbed to their own evil desires. Even when confronted with the truth, their hearts remained hardened. Nearly everyone in the dream had fallen into deception.

God instructed me within the dream to warn the people and inform them of the spiritual battle taking place for the salvation of souls. He had granted me the ability to perceive what others couldn't, enabling me to assist them. His desire was for me to prepare people for His imminent return. God placed a Book in my hand, urging me to run with it. I sprinted fervently, clutching the Word of God, knowing that I was called to be a spiritual sprinter, ordained by God. He spoke to me, saying, "I ran with the football, I ran with the Baton, and now it's time for me to run with the word of God." I understood that I would spend the rest of my days running for Him – as His spiritual sprinter.

He then directed my attention to a scripture passage, Habakkuk 2:3, which states, "Then the LORD answered me and said: 'Write the vision and make it plain on tablets, that he may run who reads it. For the vision is yet for an appointed time; but at the end it will speak, and it will not lie. Though it tarries, wait for it; because it will surely come. It will not tarry'" (NKJV). Although the natural world appeared calm, a fierce spiritual war raged on, invisible to the eyes of people. I was sent by God to raise my voice and sound the alarm that Jesus is coming back, and He is the only way to salvation.

PHASE 4

It is my desire for you to grow deeper in your relationship with Jesus Christ, just as I have. I have had a long road to my Damascus-like experience, but I am no different than you.

If God did it for me, He can do the same for you, for He is no respecter of persons. Like Saul, I was an unlikely candidate, and my life took a radical turn when I encountered Jesus Christ.

In fact, Saul, who later became Paul, was initially on a mission to persecute Christians when he had a powerful encounter with Jesus on his way to Damascus. Struck with blindness for three days, he emerged from that experience with a new name and identity in Christ Jesus. As the scales fell from his eyes, not only did his physical sight get restored, but his spiritual eyes were also opened. Once Paul saw the light (Jesus Christ), he was never the same.

I believe God wants to open your eyes just like He did for Paul, to bring you into the reality that Jesus Christ is the truth, the way, and the life. I want to invite you into my private time where God speaks to me in the garden of my heart—where I am alone, naked, and able to hear Him without any outside voices, including my own. My goal is to share my personal experiences with you in hopes of bringing revelation, understanding, deliverance, and increasing your appetite for Jesus Christ.

Perhaps you, too, have had dreams and visions, and you might wonder if they are from God or just your imagination. I learned that God uses our imagination to communicate with us, and it is a powerful tool for creativity and receiving divine inspiration. Imagination has led to groundbreaking inventions and innovations throughout history.

As I grew in my walk with Christ, I discovered that my dreams, visions, and encounters were not just imaginary experiences (see Acts 2:17). God drew me closer and revealed the reality of the spiritual world that I was once blinded to. I realized that this natural world is fleeting, and the true reality lives in the eternal. Many people, including Christians, remain ignorant of this reality because they have not encountered it yet.

We all need to experience the seer realm and encounter the Holy Spirit. For me, deliverance was tied up in the spirit. It wasn't until the Holy Spirit opened my eyes and revealed this truth that I was able to receive my deliverance. I no longer fought an unseen enemy; God opened the dimensions of the seer realm to me. I had to pray, fast, renounce, and walk through my deliverance process. If you face similar roadblocks like pornography, fear, fear of man, or rejection, I want to share some unique strategies God has given me that helped me receive wholeness.

OVERCOMING PORNOGRAPHY

I battled with pornography for more than 10 years. I tried to break free from it on many occasions, reading self-help books and keeping track of streaks of days without watching, but somehow I always found myself right back in that pit. It wasn't until God revealed that my addiction was spiritual that I began to deal with the root of my addiction in the spirit.

The first instruction God gave me was too fast. I fasted away from social media, cell phone, and any visual devices that would tempt me. During my fast, I went through renunciation and read deliverance books, such as "Prayers that Rout Demons" by John Eckhardt. I spent countless hours praying in the spirit.

When this was all over, I felt much lighter and freer than I had ever been. My mind was clear, and I didn't have to live in constant condemnation. I had to pray and free myself from feelings of rejection, abandonment, loneliness, and isolation, which were also part of the root cause of why I was watching pornography.

As part of the process, I had to heal and patch up my relationship with my mother so that there would be no voids or reasons to go back to pornography. Rejection is often the root cause of pornography.

Even after completing my fast, I still had to maintain my deliverance. The urges weren't as strong, but the knocks were still there. I had to choose whether or not to open that door back up again.

Most importantly, we all need the help of the Holy Spirit to maintain our deliverance. We would be foolish to think that we can maintain our deliverance on our own. We must learn to live a life yielded to the holy spirit by following his lead daily. The apostle Paul stated, "I affirm, by the boasting in you which I have in Christ Jesus our Lord, I die daily" (1 Corinthians 15:31 NKJV). One must choose to stay free by crucifying the flesh every day.

Deliverance is an ongoing process one must choose to stay delivered.

DISMANTLING FEAR & ANXIETY

Fear is a peculiar form of worship, as it possesses the ability to speak to you. When fear gains access to your heart, it also infiltrates your mind. Fear is not something you inherently inherit; it is taught through various means, such as nightmares, molestation, and trauma.

Nightmares can often be seen as coaching sessions with fear. Like me, one of the greatest hurdles I had to overcome was fear and anxiety. I recall a morning when I woke up, on my way to work, and God granted me a vivid vision depicting the essence of fear. In this vision, I saw a man with a black mist suspended above his head.

At that moment, the Lord posed a question to me, "How does fear acquire its power?"

I replied, "I don't know, Lord."

Then, the Holy Spirit spoke, describing fear as a parasite that only wields power when you empower it. This revelation prompted me to delve into researching parasites, their functions, and their connection to fear. During my research, I stumbled upon some valuable insights. A parasite is an organism that dwells in or on another species (its host) and benefits by deriving nutrients at the expense of the host. It symbolizes someone who habitually exploits or relies on others without reciprocation—think freeloaders, leeches, and bloodsuckers.

Fear, the metaphorical parasite, takes and gives nothing in return. It solely affects the host, unable to grow without the host's sustenance. The parasite depends on the host for survival. Picture yourself as the host, and fear as the parasite—it can only enter if you invite it in. Nevertheless, as believers, we possess the power to evict fear. As it is written in 2 Timothy 1:7, "For God hath not given us the spirit of fear, but of power and of love and of a sound mind."(KJV) Demons are nourished by what they consume, and while they cannot feed themselves, you have the capacity to feed them. Their goal is to sow a seed of fear within you to manifest itself and, more significantly, to propagate fear among those around you. To achieve this, they need a conducive environment for the parasite to thrive.

You may be wondering what this environment looks like. The answer is simple: wherever there is a ready supply of fear (parasites), that is where they reside. The environment caters to the appetite of the attached demon. Therefore, the longer you succumb to fear, the longer it exerts control over you. It is superficial to believe that the enemy's aim is solely to harm you with fear. His agenda extends further, aiming to implant fear within you to eventually influence those around you, creating a community of fearful individuals.

Breaking the agreement with fear in your life is crucial. Moreover, it's important to recognize that fear can assume various forms. It adapts to be whatever it needs to be. Whatever you fear, that is the form fear takes on—whether it's the fear of marriage, divorce, abandonment, or any other manifestation. Consider this analogy: if I use my hand to create a shadow on a wall and shine light upon it, it may resemble a terrifying animal. However, in reality, it is merely the shadow of my hand. Ignorantly, I didn't realize it was just an illusion; it was never what I thought it was.

Fear is akin to a shadow. In Psalm 23:4, it is written, "Yea, though I walk through the valley of the shadow of death, I will fear no evil: for thou art with me; thy rod and thy staff they comfort me" (KJV).

God will never abandon or forsake you. He will not allow fear to consume you; instead, He will deliver and comfort you in times of trouble. It's important to know that when you are dismantling fear (Parasite) it's not enough just to tell it to leave. You must command the spirit of fear to leave, and you must get rid of everything it's using to cling onto in order to remain in your life. If there is no food to eat the parasite cannot survive in that environment.

You have to begin to eat the word of God daily. Fill yourself with the truth of God's spoken word, and allow it to be rooted in your heart. When fear begins to speak to you the word of God will be like a double edged sword in your mouth piercing the lies of the enemy. Once the spirit of fear (parasite) is removed now God can begin to reprogram your heart. The love of God is the antidote to fear. One cannot fully embrace the love of God, with fear programmed in their heart. Remember, God has not given us a spirit of fear, but of power and of love and of a sound mind (2 Timothy 2:7). There is no fear in love, but perfect love casts out fear. For fear has to do with punishment, and whoever fears has not been perfected in love (John 4:18). When fear is removed now God's love can be perfected in your heart.

FINAL THOUGHTS

I am a man of encounters, and I share with you not something I've merely read about in the life of another, but my own personal experiences with the Lord. My intention is not to seek fame or glory for myself; my sole purpose is to glorify Jesus Christ and use my life's testimony as a compass to point you toward Him.

My dear brothers and sisters, God does not want you to live vicariously through my experiences or anyone else's. Instead, He longs for you to have your own personal relationship, encounters, visitations, and experiences with Him. He placed a mandate upon me to share my experiences with the world so that many would believe.

Beloved, if it were solely up to me, I would have kept these encounters and experiences to myself. However, that is not what Jesus wants. Dear brothers and sisters, our God is a God of multiplication, a principle evident throughout Scripture. Just as Jesus commanded the disciples in Matthew 28:19-20 to multiply by making disciples of all nations. I know, because He told me; and I have Isaiah's example when he said, "Here am I. Send me!" (Isaiah 6:8).

This is the kind of response God desires from all of us. Here I am, Lord, send me! God seeks those who are willing and obedient. He does not desire to grant you encounters so you can boast, brag, or become prideful. Instead, He wants you to testify to help win the lost, freeing people from the shackles of religion; freeing them from anything that hinders their growth and fully believing and embracing the deeper things of God. Remember that Jesus couldn't perform miracles in His own hometown due to their unbelief (Matthew 13:58).

Before God can elevate you to this realm, you must confront any unbelief that may be hidden in your heart towards these divine experiences. This is important because once Jesus opens your eyes and begins revealing heavenly things to you – you will never view the world the same. You will no longer see things through filters of your desires, but rather, you will see them as they truly are.

Also know, with new revelation and knowledge comes great responsibility. This is why God withholds some encounters until you have reached a certain level of maturity in him. This saying is common, and weighs true: to whom much is given, much is required. Once you have the knowledge, you are responsible for it.

The weight of responsibility can suffocate a person if they are not ready. It is God's mercy to not expose you to the deeper things until the appointed time.

* * *

This is the good news of the Gospel: The kingdom of heaven has come to earth. If you're reading this and you have not accepted Jesus Christ into your heart, here's an opportunity for you to do so. Romans 10:9 makes it plain, "If you declare with your mouth, 'Jesus is Lord,' and believe in your heart that God raised him from the dead, you will be saved."

I want you to stop what you're doing and pray this prayer:

Jesus, I humbly come before you acknowledging that I am a sinner. I repent for all of my sins and ask for your forgiveness. I believe that you died and were raised from the dead so that I might have eternal life. Jesus I invite you into my heart as my savior, and ask that you would be the lord of my life"

Congratulations, you're now a born-again believer! You have been washed clean, and all your sins have been washed away. "Therefore, if anyone is in Christ, the new creation has come: The old has gone, the new is here!" (2 Corinthians 5:17 NIV) Your salvation is complete.

Now the next phase is to walk out your sanctification. It is up to you to build your relationship with Christ. Don't worry about striving for perfection, just know that God's perfect Spirit now dwells inside of you.

Take it day by day and allow the Holy Spirit (the Spirit of Truth) to lead you along your journey. Always remember, we're all saved by Grace and not by our works. It's not a payout; it's a gift. Don't be tempted into working for righteousness. We are all saved through Christ Jesus, and it is not earned. It is a gift. There's nothing that we could do on this earth to earn salvation. The only guarantee we have is to lean on the grace and mercies of God.

Outside of receiving salvation, the baptism of the holy spirit is the best thing that has ever happened to me. My encounter with the Holy Spirit has changed my entire life. It is my friend and my constant companion.

John 14:15-31 explains this to us, "And I will ask the Father, and he will give you another advocate to help you and be with you forever the Spirit of truth. The world cannot accept him, because it neither sees him nor knows him. But you know him, for he lives with you and will be with you."

How can we say we love God and ignore the one he sent (the person of the Holy spirit)? Jesus is now seated at the right hand of the father, and the Holy Spirit was sent in his stead to aid us in this life (Mark 16:19).

Baptism is the outward declaration of repentance. It signifies your decision to surrender your life to the Lord and turn away from self, sin, and the world, fully embracing Jesus. It's not enough to confess your sins, but you must also forsake them. Peter replied, "Repent and be baptized, every one of you, in the name of Jesus Christ for the forgiveness of your sins. And you will receive the gift of the Holy Spirit" (Acts 2:38 NIV).

When God's power comes upon a believer it enables you to remain free from sin, live righteously, and serve with strength. "We are witnesses of these things, and so is the Holy Spirit, whom God has given to those who obey him" (Acts 2:32 NIV).

The second phase involves living a surrendered life in obedience to God's will for you. Once you've repented and are obedient to God, the subsequent step is seeking the baptism of the Holy Spirit.

Now there is a difference between initially receiving the Holy Spirit versus the baptism of the Holy Spirit with signs and wonders as evidence. Every believer is initially filled with the holy spirit at salvation. However, the baptism of (fire) the Holy Spirit does not always happen at the door of salvation. For example the distinction between being filled and being consumed or submerged lies in the outcome. When something is filled, the vessel remains intact; however, when something is consumed, the vessel becomes one with the substance it's submerged into. Imagine filling a bottle with water—the vessel remains intact. Conversely, if you place a vessel on fire or submerge it in blank ink, the vessel vanishes into the substance. It's overtaken both within and without. When you receive the baptism of (fire) the Holy Spirit, a transformation occurs that defies staying unchanged.

John 20:19-23 recounts, "On the evening of that first day of the week, when the disciples were together, with the doors locked for fear of the Jewish leaders, Jesus came and stood among them and said, 'Peace be with you!' After he said this, he showed them his hands and side. The disciples were overjoyed when they saw the Lord. Again Jesus said, 'Peace be with you! As the Father has sent me, I am sending you.' And with that, he breathed on them and said, 'Receive the Holy Spirit.'"(NIV)

After Jesus' resurrection, He appeared to the disciples and they received the Holy Spirit. However, Jesus still instructed them to await the baptism (power) of the Holy Spirit. Acts chapter two describes the Pentecost event, where the were filled with the Holy Spirit and spoke in tongues as the Spirit enabled them. Before Jesus commissioned the disciples, they waited in the upper room for ten days. This concept is mirrored in the life of Jesus during His baptism by John the Baptist.

Mark 1:9-11 details Jesus' baptism in the Jordan River: "It came to pass in those days that Jesus came from Nazareth of Galilee and was baptized by John in the Jordan. And immediately, coming up from the water, he saw the heavens parting and the Spirit descending on him like a dove. Then a voice came from heaven, 'You are my beloved Son, in whom I am well pleased.' Immediately the Spirit drove him into the wilderness. And he was there in the wilderness forty days, tempted by Satan and was with the wild beasts; and the angels ministered to Him"(NKJV). Jesus emerged from baptism, affirmed by the Father, but didn't immediately start preaching. Instead, He was led by the Spirit into the wilderness to prepare for forty days and receive the power of the Holy Spirit.

Luke 4:14-15 (NKJV) notes, "Then Jesus returned in the power of the Spirit to Galilee, and news of Him went out through all the surrounding region. And He taught in their synagogues, being glorified by all." Jesus paid the price to receive the power of the Holy Spirit. Similarly, the baptism of the Spirit isn't granted automatically to every believer; there's a price to be paid. Jesus waited in the wilderness for forty days and nights, and the apostles waited in the upper room for ten days, unaware of the exact moment the Holy Spirit would come. In my personal experience, I was directed to leave everything behind in Dallas and relocate to Houston. I had no idea why, but I followed the Holy Spirit's lead in obedience. Forsaking all and following Jesus was my cost.

God had a divine plan that required my obedience. Many Christians mistakenly believe that God's promises unfold automatically, but that's not true. We must align with His plans through obedience. I found myself in a storefront church in Houston, encountering the (Person) Holy Spirit. It took about a year and a half after moving to Houston for this to happen, but the wait was well worth it.

Beloved, preaching and teaching without the power of the Holy Spirit is mere religion, while walking in the Holy Spirit's power is kingdom living. 1 Corinthians 4:20 reminds us that the kingdom of God is not a matter of talk but of power. Once Jesus and the apostles received the power of the Holy Spirit, they were empowered for ministry and turned the world upside down.

As you begin your journey, it's critical to develop your relationship with the Holy spirit. Jesus told the disciples that it is the work of the Holy spirit to teach and remind you of everything I have told you (See John 14:26). The Holy Spirit never speaks on his own, but what's given to him by Jesus. John 16:14 states, He will glorify me because it is from me that he will receive what he will make known to you.

Beloved, learn to strive with the Holy Spirit and he will make Jesus known to you. As the Spirit of the Lord has given me the tongue of the learned and the pen of a ready writer, I share my experiences with you so that your faith might increase. It is my deepest desire that your spiritual eyes and the understanding of your heart be opened.

May the same grace that God has given me to be a man of deep encounters be imparted into your life today; and may the flame of the Spirit continue to burn within you for the rest of your days. Shalom.

ABOUT THE AUTHOR

Prophet Jonathan Emmanuel Davis, overseer at Eden Ministries, is on a divine mission to spread the gospel and kingdom message worldwide. As an apostolic prophet, he carries a special message from Jesus, focusing on the profound importance of relationship with Him.

Residing in Dallas, TX with his wife, Mojana Davis, and son, Elijah Davis, he is known for being a man of the presence, his revelatory insights, and divine encounters.

www.ingramcontent.com/pod-product-compliance
Lightning Source LLC
Chambersburg PA
CBHW071752120626
46550CB00002B/765

* 9 7 9 8 9 8 9 5 6 5 5 3 5 *